OPEN ACCESS

PETER SUBER

The MIT Press | Cambridge, Massachusetts | London, England

MIT Press books may be purchased at special quantity discounts for business or sales promotional use. For information, please email special_sales@ mitpress.mit.edu or write to Special Sales Department, The MIT Press, 55 Hayward Street, Cambridge, MA 02142.

This book was set in Chaparral Pro by the MIT Press and was printed and bound in the United States of America.

Library of Congress Cataloging-in-Publication Data

Suber, Peter.
Open access / Peter Suber.
   p.   cm. — (MIT Press essential knowledge)
Includes bibliographical references and index.
ISBN 978-0-262-51763-8 (pbk. : alk. paper)
1. Open access publishing. I. Title.
Z286.O63S83   2012
070.5'7973—dc23

                                                                                2011038297

10   9   8   7   6   5   4   3   2

CONTENTS

SERIES FOREWORD

The MIT Press Essential Knowledge series presents short, accessible books on need-to-know subjects in a variety of fields. Written by leading thinkers, Essential Knowledge volumes deliver concise, expert overviews of topics ranging from the cultural and historical to the scientific and technical. In our information age, opinion, rationalization, and superficial descriptions are readily available. Much harder to come by are the principled understanding and foundational knowledge needed to inform our opinions and decisions. This series of beautifully produced, pocket-sized, soft-cover books provides in-depth, authoritative material on topics of current interest in a form accessible to non-experts. Instead of condensed versions of specialist texts, these books synthesize anew important subjects for a knowledgeable audience. For those who seek to enter a subject via its fundamentals, Essential Knowledge volumes deliver the understanding and insight needed to navigate a complex world.

Bruce Tidor
Professor of Biological Engineering and Computer Science
Massachusetts Institute of Technology

PREFACE

I have worked full-time for a decade to foster open access (OA) to science and scholarship. During that time I have often boiled down the big message into short talks and written long articles exploring small subtopics in detail. This book is an attempt at something in between: a succinct introduction to the basics, long enough to cover the major topics in reasonable detail and short enough for busy people to read.

I want busy people to read this book. OA benefits literally everyone, for the same reasons that research itself benefits literally everyone. OA performs this service by facilitating research and making the results more widely available and useful. It benefits researchers as readers by helping them find and retrieve the information they need, and it benefits researchers as authors by helping them reach readers who can apply, cite, and build on their work. OA benefits nonresearchers by accelerating research and all the goods that depend on research, such as new medicines, useful technologies, solved problems, informed decisions, improved policies, and beautiful understanding.

But OA only does this good work insofar as we actually implement it, and the people in a position to implement it tend to be busy. I'm thinking about researchers themselves and policymakers at stakeholder institutions such as universities, libraries, publishers, scholarly societies, funding agencies, and governments.

My honest belief from experience in the trenches is that the largest obstacle to OA is misunderstanding. The largest cause of misunderstanding is lack of familiarity, and the largest cause of unfamiliarity is preoccupation. Everyone is busy. There has been organized opposition from some publishers, but that has been a minor impediment by comparison.

The best remedy to misunderstanding is a clear statement of the basics for busy people. Only some fellow specialists will wonder, with me, whether I've been too brief with some essential subtopics. But I knew that a larger book would miss the audience of busy people. Elaboration, documentation, research findings, case studies, and finergrained recommendations are available in the voluminous literature online (most of it OA), including my own articles (all of them OA).[1]

This book will itself be OA twelve months after it appears in print. (I'm glad you asked.) If you can't wait, everything I've said here I've said in some form or another in an OA article.

I have freely incorporated some relevant earlier writings into this book, improving on them when I could. Notes at the end of the book indicate which pieces I adapted or incorporated into which sections. I chose this method as a solution to a pair of dilemmas. I did not want to hide the fact that I was making use of my previous work, but neither did I want to make any section into a stream of self-quotation and self-citation. I did not want to fail to benefit from my own previous work, but neither did I want to miss opportunities to clarify, update, or improve it.

This little book doesn't say much about kindred topics such as open data, open educational resources, open government, free and open-source software, or open science (combining OA texts, open data, and open-source software, and providing these sorts of openness at every stage of a research project, not just at the end in reporting results). Some of the kindred forms of scholarly openness might soon be covered by other volumes in this series.

I would not have been able to give my full time to OA for so many years without grants from the Open Society Foundations, Wellcome Trust, and Arcadia and without financial or institutional support from Earlham College, Public Knowledge, the Scholarly Publishing and Academic Resources Coalition (SPARC), the University of Maine, Data Conversion Laboratory, the Information Society Project at Yale Law School, the Berkman Center for Internet & Society at Harvard University, the Harvard Law School Library, and the Harvard Office for Scholarly Communication. For their generous support for OA and my work I thank Fay Bound Alberti, Peter Baldwin, Jack Balkin,

Douglas Bennett, Len Clark, Darius Cuplinskas, Robert Darnton, Urs Gasser, Melissa Hagemann, Rick Johnson, Heather Joseph, Robert Kiley, Sue Kriegsman, Harlan Onsrud, John Palfrey, Lisbet Rausing, Stuart Shieber, David Skurnik, and Gigi Sohn.

I dedicate this book to the thousands of people in every field and country who have dedicated themselves to the realization of OA. The ones I know personally are already too numerous to thank by name in the preface to a short book, and the fact that there are more than I could thank by name—even if I tried—fills me with admiration, gratitude, and optimism.

*Please also see Peter Suber's online page of updates and supplements to this book at http://bit.ly/oa-book.

WHAT IS OPEN ACCESS?

Shifting from ink on paper to digital text suddenly allows us to make perfect copies of our work. Shifting from isolated computers to a globe-spanning network of connected computers suddenly allows us to share perfect copies of our work with a worldwide audience at essentially no cost. About thirty years ago this kind of free global sharing became something new under the sun. Before that, it would have sounded like a quixotic dream.

Digital technologies have created more than one revolution. Let's call this one the access revolution.

Why don't more authors take advantage of the access revolution to reach more readers? The answer is pretty clear. Authors who share their works in this way aren't selling them, and even authors with purposes higher than money depend on sales to make a living. Or at least they appreciate sales.

Let's sharpen the question, then, by putting to one side authors who want to sell their work. We can even acknowledge that we're putting aside the vast majority of authors.

Imagine a tribe of authors who write serious and useful work, and who follow a centuries-old custom of giving it away without charge. I don't mean a group of rich authors who don't need money. I mean a group of authors defined by their topics, genres, purposes, incentives, and institutional circumstances, not by their wealth. In fact, very few are wealthy. For now, it doesn't matter who these authors are, how rare they are, what they write, or why they follow this peculiar custom. It's enough to know that their employers pay them salaries, freeing them to give away their work, that they write for impact rather than money, and that they score career points when they make the kind of impact they hoped to make. Suppose that selling their work would actually harm their interests by shrinking their audience, reducing their impact, and distorting their professional goals by steering them toward popular topics and away from the specialized questions on which they are experts.

If authors like that exist, at least they should take advantage of the access revolution. The dream of global free access can be a reality for them, even if most other authors hope to earn royalties and feel obliged to sit out this particular revolution.

It's enough to know that their employers pay them salaries, freeing them to give away their work, that they write for impact rather than money, and that they score career points when they make the kind of impact they hoped to make.

These lucky authors are scholars, and the works they customarily write and publish without payment are peer-reviewed articles in scholarly journals. *Open access* is the name of the revolutionary kind of access these authors, unencumbered by a motive of financial gain, are free to provide to their readers.

> Open access (OA) literature is digital, online, free of charge, and free of most copyright and licensing restrictions.

We could call it "barrier-free" access, but that would emphasize the negative rather than the positive. In any case, we can be more specific about which access barriers OA removes.

A price tag is a significant access barrier. Most works with price tags are individually affordable. But when a scholar needs to read or consult hundreds of works for one research project, or when a library must provide access for thousands of faculty and students working on tens of thousands of topics, and when the volume of new work grows explosively every year, price barriers become insurmountable. The resulting access gaps harm authors by limiting their audience and impact, harm readers by limiting what they can retrieve and read, and thereby harm research from both directions. OA removes price barriers.

Copyright can also be a significant access barrier. If you have access to a work for reading but want to translate it into another language, distribute copies to colleagues, copy the text for mining with sophisticated software, or reformat it for reading with new technology, then you generally need the permission of the copyright holder. That makes sense when the author wants to sell the work and when the use you have in mind could undermine sales. But for research articles we're generally talking about authors from the special tribe who want to share their work as widely as possible. Even these authors, however, tend to transfer their copyrights to intermediaries—publishers—who want to sell their work. As a result, users may be hampered in their research by barriers erected to serve intermediaries rather than authors. In addition, replacing user freedom with permission-seeking harms research authors by limiting the usefulness of their work, harms research readers by limiting the uses they may make of works even when they have access, and thereby harms research from both directions. OA removes these permission barriers.

Removing price barriers means that readers are not limited by their own ability to pay, or by the budgets of the institutions where they may have library privileges. Removing permission barriers means that scholars are free to use or reuse literature for scholarly purposes. These purposes include reading and searching, but also redistributing, translating, text mining, migrating to new media,

Terminology

When we need to, we can be more specific about access vehicles and access barriers. In the jargon, OA delivered by journals is called *gold OA*, and OA delivered by repositories is called *green OA*. Work that is not open access, or that is available only for a price, is called *toll access* (TA). Over the years I've asked publishers for a neutral, nonpejorative and nonhonorific term for toll-access publishers, and *conventional publishers* is the suggestion I hear most often. While every kind of OA removes price barriers, there are many different permission barriers we could remove if we wanted to. If we remove price barriers alone, we provide *gratis OA*, and if we remove at least some permission barriers as well, we provide *libre OA*. (Also see section 3.1 on green/gold and section 3.3 on gratis/libre.)

long-term archiving, and innumerable new forms of research, analysis, and processing we haven't yet imagined. OA makes work more useful in both ways, by making it available to more people who can put it to use, and by freeing those people to use and reuse it.

OA was defined in three influential public statements: the Budapest Open Access Initiative (February 2002), the Bethesda Statement on Open Access Publishing (June 2003), and the Berlin Declaration on Open Access to Knowledge in the Sciences and Humanities (October 2003).[1] I sometimes refer to their overlap or common ground as the BBB definition of OA. My definition here is the BBB definition reduced to its essential elements and refined with some post-BBB terminology (green, gold, gratis, libre) for speaking precisely about subspecies of OA. Here's how the Budapest statement defined OA:

> There are many degrees and kinds of wider and easier access to [research] literature. By "open access" to this literature, we mean its free availability on the public internet, permitting any users to read, download, copy, distribute, print, search, or link to the full texts of these articles, crawl them for indexing, pass them as data to software, or use them for any other lawful purpose, without financial, legal, or technical barriers other than those inseparable from gaining access to the internet itself. The only constraint on reproduction and distribution, and the only role for copyright in this domain, should be to give authors control over the integrity of their work and the right to be properly acknowledged and cited.

Here's how the Bethesda and Berlin statements put it: For a work to be OA, the copyright holder must consent in advance to let users "copy, use, distribute, transmit and display the work publicly and to make and distribute derivative works, in any digital medium for any responsible purpose, subject to proper attribution of authorship."

Note that all three legs of the BBB definition go beyond removing price barriers to removing permission barriers, or beyond gratis OA to libre OA. But at the same time, all three allow at least one limit on user freedom: an obligation to attribute the work to the author. The purpose of OA is to remove barriers to all legitimate scholarly uses for scholarly literature, but there's no legitimate scholarly purpose in suppressing attribution to the texts we use. (That's why my shorthand definition says that OA literature is free of "most" rather than "all" copyright and licensing restrictions.)

The basic idea of OA is simple: Make research literature available online without price barriers and without most permission barriers. Even the implementation is simple enough that the volume of peer-reviewed OA literature and the number of institutions providing it have grown at an increasing rate for more than a decade. If there are complexities, they lie in the transition from where we are now to a world in which OA is the default for new research. This is complicated because the major obstacles are not technical, legal, or economic, but cultural. (More in chapter 9 on the future.)[2]

In principle, any kind of digital content can be OA, since any digital content can be put online without price or permission barriers. Moreover, any kind of content can be digital: texts, data, images, audio, video, multimedia, and executable code. We can have OA music and movies, news and novels, sitcoms and software—and to different degrees we already do. But the term "open access" was coined by researchers trying to remove access barriers to research. The next section explains why.

1.1   What Makes OA Possible?[3]

OA is made possible by the internet and copyright-holder consent. But why would a copyright holder consent to OA?

Two background facts suggest the answer. First, authors are the copyright holders for their work until or unless they transfer rights to someone else, such as a publisher.

Second, scholarly journals generally don't pay authors for their research articles, which frees this special tribe of authors to consent to OA without losing revenue. This fact distinguishes scholars decisively from musicians and moviemakers, and even from most other kinds of authors. This is why controversies about OA to music and movies don't carry over to OA for research articles.

Both facts are critical, but the second is nearly unknown outside the academic world. It's not a new fact of academic life, arising from a recent economic downturn in the publishing industry. Nor is it a case of corporate exploitation of unworldly academics. Scholarly journals haven't paid authors for their articles since the first scholarly journals, the *Philosophical Transactions* of the Royal Society of London and the *Journal des sçavans*, launched in London and Paris in 1665.[4]

The academic custom to write research articles for impact rather than money may be a lucky accident that could have been otherwise. Or it may be a wise adaptation that would eventually evolve in any culture with a serious research subculture. (The optimist in me wants to believe the latter, but the evolution of copyright law taunts that optimism.) This peculiar custom does more than insulate cutting-edge research from the market and free scholars to consent to OA without losing revenue. It also supports academic freedom and the kinds of serious inquiry that advance knowledge. It frees researchers to challenge conventional wisdom and defend unpopular ideas, which are essential to academic freedom. At the same time it frees them to microspecialize and defend ideas of immediate interest to just a handful people in the world, which are essential to pushing the frontiers of knowledge.

This custom doesn't guarantee that truth-seeking won't be derailed by profit-seeking, and it doesn't guarantee

The academic custom to write research articles for impact rather than money may be a lucky accident that could have been otherwise. Or it may be a wise adaptation that would eventually evolve in any culture with a serious research subculture.

that we'll eventually fill the smallest gaps in our collaborative understanding of the world. It doesn't even guarantee that scholars won't sometimes play for the crowd and detour into fad thinking. But it removes a major distraction by allowing them, if they wish, to focus on what is likely to be true rather than what is likely to sell. It's a payment structure we need for good research itself, not just for good access to research, and it's the key to the legal and economic lock that would otherwise shackle steps toward OA.

Creative people who live by royalties, such as novelists, musicians, and moviemakers, may consider this scholarly tradition a burden and sacrifice for scholars. We might even agree, provided we don't overlook a few facts. First, it's a sacrifice that scholars have been making for nearly 350 years. OA to research articles doesn't depend on asking royalty-earning authors to give up their royalties. Second, academics have salaries from universities, freeing them to dive deeply into their research topics and publish specialized articles without market appeal. Many musicians and moviemakers might envy that freedom to disregard sales and popular taste. Third, academics receive other, less tangible rewards from their institutions—like promotion and tenure—when their research is recognized by others, accepted, cited, applied, and built upon.

It's no accident that faculty who advance knowledge in their fields also advance their careers. Academics are passionate about certain topics, ideas, questions, inquiries, or disciplines. They feel lucky to have jobs in which they may pursue these passions and even luckier to be rewarded for pursuing them. Some focus single-mindedly on carrying an honest pebble to the pile of knowledge (as John Lange put it), having an impact on their field, or scooping others working on the same questions. Others focus strategically on building the case for promotion and tenure. But the two paths converge, which is not a fortuitous fact of nature but an engineered fact of life in the academy. As incentives for productivity, these intangible career benefits may be stronger for the average researcher than royalties are for the average novelist or musician. (In both domains, bountiful royalties for superstars tell us nothing about effective payment models for the long tail of less stellar professionals.)

There's no sense in which research would be more free, efficient, or effective if academics took a more "businesslike" position, behaved more like musicians and moviemakers, abandoned their insulation from the market, and tied their income to the popularity of their ideas. Nonacademics who urge academics to come to their senses and demand royalties even for journal articles may be more naive about nonprofit research than academics are about for-profit business.[5]

We can take this a step further. Scholars can afford to ignore sales because they have salaries and research grants to take the place of royalties. But why do universities pay salaries and why do funding agencies award grants? They do it to advance research and the range of public interests served by research. They don't do it to earn profits from the results. They are all nonprofit. They certainly don't do it to make scholarly writings into gifts to enrich publishers, especially when conventional publishers erect access barriers at the expense of research. Universities and funding agencies pay researchers to make their research into gifts to the public in the widest sense.

Public and private funding agencies are essentially public and private charities, funding research they regard as useful or beneficial. Universities have a public purpose as well, even when they are private institutions. We support the public institutions with public funds, and we support the private ones with tax exemptions for their property and tax deductions for their donors.

We'd have less knowledge, less academic freedom, and less OA if researchers worked for royalties and made their research articles into commodities rather than gifts. It should be no surprise, then, that more and more funding agencies and universities are adopting strong OA policies. Their mission to advance research leads them directly to logic of OA: With a few exceptions, such as classified research, research that is worth funding or facilitating is worth sharing with everyone who can make use of it. (See chapter 4 on OA policies.)

Newcomers to OA often assume that OA helps readers and hurts authors, and that the reader side of the scholarly soul must beg the author side to make the necessary sacrifice. But OA benefits authors as well as readers. Authors want access to readers at least as much as readers want access to authors. All authors want to cultivate a larger audience and greater impact. Authors who work for royalties have reason to compromise and settle for the smaller audience of paying customers. But authors who aren't paid for their writing have no reason to compromise.

It takes nothing away from a disinterested desire to advance knowledge to recognize that scholarly publication is accompanied by a strong interest in impact and career building. The result is a mix of interested and disinterested motives. The reasons to make work OA are essentially the same as the reasons to publish. Authors who make their work OA are always serving others but not always acting from altruism. In fact, the idea that OA depends on author altruism slows down OA progress by hiding the role of author self-interest.

Another aspect of author self-interest emerges from the well-documented phenomenon that OA articles are cited more often than non-OA articles, even when they are published in the same issue of the same journal. There's growing evidence that OA articles are downloaded more often as well, and that journals converting to OA see a rise in their submissions and citation impact.[6]

There are many hypotheses to explain the correlation between OA and increased citations, but it's likely that ongoing studies will show that much of the correlation is simply due to the larger audience and heightened visibility provided by OA itself. When you enlarge the audience for an article, you also enlarge the subset of the audience that will later cite it, including professionals in the same field at institutions unable to afford subscription access. OA enlarges the potential audience, including the potential professional audience, far beyond that for even the most prestigious and popular subscription journals.

In any case, these studies bring a welcome note of author self-interest to the case for OA. OA is not a sacrifice for authors who write for impact rather than money. It increases a work's visibility, retrievability, audience, usage, and citations, which all convert to career building. For publishing scholars, it would be a bargain even if it were costly, difficult, and time-consuming. But as we'll see, it's not costly, not difficult, and not time-consuming.

My colleague Stevan Harnad frequently compares research articles to advertisements. They advertise the author's research. Try telling advertisers that they're making a needless sacrifice by allowing people to read their ads without having to pay for the privilege. Advertisers give away their ads and even pay to place them where they might be seen. They do this to benefit themselves, and scholars have the same interest in sharing their message as widely as possible.[7]

Because any content can be digital, and any digital content can be OA, OA needn't be limited to royalty-free literature like research articles. Research articles are just ripe examples of low-hanging fruit. OA could extend to royalty-producing work like monographs, textbooks, novels, news, music, and movies. But as soon as we cross the line into OA for royalty-producing work, authors will either lose revenue or fear that they will lose revenue. Either way, they'll be harder to persuade. But instead of concluding that royalty-producing work is off limits to OA, we should merely conclude that it's higher-hanging fruit. In many cases we can still persuade royalty-earning authors to consent to OA. (See section 5.3 on OA for books.)

Authors of scholarly research articles aren't the only players who work without pay in the production of research literature. In general, scholarly journals don't pay editors or referees either. In general, editors and referees are paid salaries by universities to free them, like authors, to donate their time and labor to ensure the quality of new work appearing in scholarly journals. An important consequence follows. All the key players in peer review can consent to OA without losing revenue. OA needn't dispense with peer review or favor unrefereed manuscripts over refereed articles. We can aim for the prize of OA to peer-reviewed scholarship. (See section 5.1 on peer review.)

Of course, conventional publishers are not as free as authors, editors, and referees to forgo revenue. This is a central fact in the transition to OA, and it explains why the interests of scholars and conventional publishers diverge more in the digital age than they diverged earlier. But not all publishers are conventional, and not all conventional publishers will carry print-era business models into the digital age.

Academic publishers are not monolithic. Some new ones were born OA and some older ones have completely converted to OA. Many provide OA to some of their work but not all of it. Some are experimenting with OA, and some are watching the experiments of others. Most allow green OA (through repositories) and a growing number offer at least some kind of gold OA (through journals). Some are supportive, some undecided, some opposed. Among the opposed, some have merely decided not to provide OA themselves, while others lobby actively against policies to encourage or require OA. Some oppose gold but not green OA, while others oppose green but not gold OA.

OA gains nothing and loses potential allies by blurring these distinctions. This variety reminds us (to paraphrase Tim O'Reilly) that OA doesn't threaten publishing; it only threatens existing publishers who do not adapt.[8]

A growing number of journal publishers have chosen business models allowing them to dispense with subscription revenue and offer OA. They have expenses but they also have revenue to cover their expenses. In fact, some

OA publishers are for-profit and profitable. (See chapter 7 on economics.)

Moreover, peer review is done by dedicated volunteers who don't care how a journal pays its bills, or even whether the journal is in the red or the black. If all peer-reviewed journals converted to OA overnight, the authors, editors, and referees would have the same incentives to participate in peer review that they had the day before. They needn't stop offering their services, needn't lower their standards, and needn't make sacrifices they weren't already making. They volunteer their time not because of a journal's choice of business model but because of its contribution to research. They could carry on with solvent or insolvent subscription publishers, with solvent or insolvent OA publishers, or even without publishers.

The Budapest Open Access Initiative said in February 2002: "An old tradition and a new technology have converged to make possible an unprecedented public good. The old tradition is the willingness of scientists and scholars to publish the fruits of their research in scholarly journals without payment.... The new technology is the internet."[9] To see what this willingness looks like without the medium to give it effect, look at scholarship in the age of print. Author gifts turned into publisher commodities, and access gaps for readers were harmfully large and widespread. (Access gaps are still harmfully large and widespread, but only because OA is not yet the default for new research.) To see what the medium looks like without the willingness, look at music and movies in the age of the internet. The need for royalties keeps creators from reaching everyone who would enjoy their work.

A beautiful opportunity exists where the willingness and the medium overlap. A scholarly custom that evolved in the seventeenth century frees scholars to take advantage of the access revolution in the twentieth and twenty-first. Because scholars are nearly unique in following this custom, they are nearly unique in their freedom to take advantage of this revolution without financial risk. In this sense, the planets have aligned for scholars. Most other authors are constrained to fear rather than seize the opportunities created by the internet.

1.2   What OA Is Not[10]

We can dispel a cloud of objections and misunderstandings simply by pointing out a few things that OA is not. (Many of these points will be elaborated in later chapters.)

1. OA isn't an attempt to bypass peer review. OA is compatible with every kind of peer review, from the most conservative to the most innovative, and all the major public statements on OA insist on its importance. Because scholarly journals generally don't pay peer-reviewing editors and referees, just as they don't pay authors, all the participants in peer review can consent to OA without losing

revenue. While OA to unrefereed preprints is useful and widespread, the OA movement isn't limited to unrefereed preprints and, if anything, focuses on OA to peer-reviewed articles. (More in section 5.1 on peer review.)

2. OA isn't an attempt to reform, violate, or abolish copyright. It's compatible with copyright law as it is. OA would benefit from the right kinds of copyright reforms, and many dedicated people are working on them. But it needn't wait for reforms and hasn't waited. OA literature avoids copyright problems in exactly the same way that conventional toll-access literature does. For older works, it takes advantage of the public domain, and for newer works, it rests on copyright-holder consent. (More in chapter 4 on policies and chapter 6 on copyright.)

3. OA isn't an attempt to deprive royalty-earning authors of income. The OA movement focuses on research articles precisely because they don't pay royalties. In any case, inside and outside that focus, OA for copyrighted work depends on copyright-holder consent. Hence, royalty-earning authors have nothing to fear but persuasion that the benefits of OA might outweigh the risks to royalties. (More in section 5.3 on OA for books.)

4. OA isn't an attempt to deny the reality of costs. No serious OA advocate has ever argued that OA literature is costless to produce, although many argue that it is less expensive to produce than conventionally published literature, even less expensive than born-digital toll-access

literature. The question is not whether research literature can be made costless, but whether there are better ways to pay the bills than charging readers and creating access barriers. (More in chapter 7 on economics.)

5. OA isn't an attempt to reduce authors' rights over their work. On the contrary, OA depends on author decisions and requires authors to exercise more rights or control over their work than they are allowed to exercise

under traditional publishing contracts. One OA strategy is for authors to retain some of the rights they formerly gave publishers, including the right to authorize OA. Another OA strategy is for publishers to permit more uses than they formerly permitted, including permission for authors to make OA copies of their work. By contrast, traditional journal-publishing contracts demand that authors transfer all rights to publishers, and author rights or control cannot sink lower than that. (See chapters 4 on policies and 6 on copyright.)

6. OA isn't an attempt to reduce academic freedom. Academic authors remain free to submit their work to the journals or publishers of their choice. Policies requiring OA do so conditionally, for example, for researchers who choose to apply for a certain kind of grant. In addition, these policies generally build in exceptions, waiver options, or both. Since 2008 most university OA policies have been adopted by faculty deeply concerned to preserve and even enhance their prerogatives. (See chapter 4 on OA policies.)

7. OA isn't an attempt to relax rules against plagiarism. All the public definitions of OA support author attribution, even construed as a "restriction" on users. All the major open licenses require author attribution. Moreover, plagiarism is typically punished by the plagiarist's institution rather than by courts, that is, by social norms rather than by law. Hence, even when attribution is not legally

required, plagiarism is still a punishable offense and no OA policy anywhere interferes with those punishments. In any case, if making literature digital and online makes plagiarism easier to commit, then OA makes plagiarism easier to detect. Not all plagiarists are smart, but the smart ones will not steal from OA sources indexed in every search engine. In this sense, OA deters plagiarism.[11]

8. OA isn't an attempt to punish or undermine conventional publishers. OA is an attempt to advance the interests of research, researchers, and research institutions. The goal is constructive, not destructive. If OA does eventually harm toll-access publishers, it will be in the way that personal computers harmed typewriter manufacturers. The harm was not the goal, but a side effect of developing something better. Moreover, OA doesn't challenge publishers or publishing per se, just one business model for publishing, and it's far easier for conventional publishers to adapt to OA than for typewriter manufacturers to adapt to computers. In fact, most toll-access publishers are already adapting, by allowing author-initiated OA, providing some OA themselves, or experimenting with OA. (See section 3.1 on green OA and chapter 8 on casualties.)[12]

9. OA doesn't require boycotting any kind of literature or publisher. It doesn't require boycotting toll-access research any more than free online journalism requires boycotting priced online journalism. OA doesn't require us to

strike toll-access literature from our personal reading lists, course syllabi, or libraries. Some scholars who support OA decide to submit new work only to OA journals, or to donate their time as editors or referees only to OA journals, in effect boycotting toll-access journals as authors, editors, and referees. But this choice is not forced by the definition of OA, by a commitment to OA, or by any OA policy, and most scholars who support OA continue to work with toll-access journals. In any case, even those scholars who do boycott toll-access journals as authors, editors, or referees don't boycott them as readers. (Here we needn't get into the complexity that some toll-access journals effectively create involuntary reader boycotts by pricing their journals out of reach of readers who want access.)

10. OA isn't primarily about bringing access to lay readers. If anything, the OA movement focuses on bringing access to professional researchers whose careers depend on access. But there's no need to decide which users are primary and which are secondary. The publishing lobby sometimes argues that the primary beneficiaries of OA are lay readers, perhaps to avoid acknowledging how many professional researchers lack access, or perhaps to set up the patronizing counter-argument that lay people don't care to read research literature and wouldn't understand it if they tried. OA is about bringing access to everyone with an internet connection who wants access, regardless of their professions or purposes. There's no doubt that if

we put "professional researchers" and "everyone else" into separate categories, a higher percentage of researchers will want access to research literature, even after taking into account that many already have paid access through their institutions. But it's far from clear why that would matter, especially when providing OA to all internet users is cheaper and simpler than providing OA to just a subset of worthy internet users.

If party-goers in New York and New Jersey can both enjoy the Fourth of July fireworks in New York Harbor, then the sponsors needn't decide that one group is primary, even if a simple study could show which group is more numerous. If this analogy breaks down, it's because New Jersey residents who can't see the fireworks gain nothing from New Yorkers who can. But research does offer this double or indirect benefit. When OA research directly benefits many lay readers, so much the better. But when it doesn't, it still benefits everyone indirectly by benefiting researchers directly. (Also see section 5.5.1 on access for lay readers.)

11. Finally, OA isn't universal access. Even when we succeed at removing price and permission barriers, four other kinds of access barrier might remain in place:

- *Filtering and censorship barriers*   Many schools, employers, ISPs, and governments want to limit what users can see.

- *Language barriers*   Most online literature is in English, or another single language, and machine translation is still very weak.

- *Handicap access barriers*   Most web sites are not yet as accessible to handicapped users as they should be.

- *Connectivity barriers*   The digital divide keeps billions of people offline, including millions of scholars, and impedes millions of others with slow, flaky, or low-bandwidth internet connections.

Most us want to remove all four of these barriers. But there's no reason to save the term *open access* until we succeed. In the long climb to universal access, removing price and permission barriers is a significant plateau worth recognizing with a special name.

MOTIVATION

2.1   OA as Solving Problems[1]

There are lamentably many problems for which OA is part of the solution. Here are fifteen ways in which the current system of disseminating peer-reviewed research is deeply dysfunctional for researchers and their institutions, even if highly profitable for the largest conventional publishers. I've limited the list to those for which OA offers some hope of relief.

1. We are in the midst of a pricing crisis for scholarly journals. For four decades, subscription prices have risen significantly faster than inflation and significantly faster than library budgets. Subscription prices have risen about twice as fast as the price of healthcare, for most people the very index of skyrocketing, unsustainable prices. We're long past the era of damage control and into the era of damage.[2]

2. When most peer-reviewed research journals are toll access, a pricing crisis entails an access crisis. Before the rise of OA, all peer-reviewed journals were toll access, and even today about three-quarters of peer-reviewed journals are toll access.[3] When subscribers respond to skyrocketing prices by canceling subscriptions, access decreases. Cancellations mitigate one problem and aggravate another. A study by the Research Information Network in late 2009 found that 40 percent of surveyed researchers had trouble accessing journal literature at least once a week, and two-thirds at least once a month. About 60 percent said that access limitations hindered their research, and 18 percent said the hindrance was significant.[4]

3. Even the wealthiest academic libraries in the world suffer serious access gaps. When the Harvard Faculty of Arts and Sciences voted unanimously for a strong OA policy in February 2008, Professor Stuart Shieber explained that cumulative price increases had forced the Harvard library to undertake "serious cancellation efforts" for budgetary reasons.[5]

Access gaps are worse at other affluent institutions, and worse still in the developing world. In 2008, Harvard subscribed to 98,900 serials and Yale to 73,900. The best-funded research library in India, at the Indian Institute of Science, subscribed to 10,600. Several sub-Saharan African university libraries subscribed to zero, offering their

Access gaps are worse at other affluent institutions, and worse still in the developing world. In 2008, Harvard subscribed to 98,900 serials and Yale to 73,900. The best-funded research library in India, at the Indian Institute of Science, subscribed to 10,600.

patrons access to no conventional journals except those donated by publishers.[6]

4. The largest publishers minimize cancellations by bundling hundreds or thousands of high-demand and low-demand journals into "big deals," which reduce the bargaining power of libraries and the cost-cutting options available to them. On the plus side, big deals give universities access to more titles than they had before and reduce the average cost per title. But when libraries try to cancel individual titles that are low in quality or low in local usage, publishers raise the price on the remaining titles. Bundling gives libraries little room to save money with carefully targeted cancellations, and after a point forces them to cancel all or none.

By design, big deals are too big to cancel without pain, giving publishers leverage to raise prices out of proportion to journal costs, size, usage, impact, and quality. Without bundling, libraries would have responded to the pricing crisis with a devastating number of cancellations. With bundling, publishers protect even second-rate journals from cancellation, protect their own profits, and shift the devastation to library budgets.[7]

While the damage grows, the largest journal publishers earn higher profit margins than the largest oil companies. In 2010, Elsevier's journal division had a profit margin of 35.7 percent while ExxonMobil had only 28.1 percent.[8]

By soaking up library budgets, big deals harm journals from small nonprofit publishers excluded from the bundles. This exacerbates the problem for researchers because journals from these smaller publishers tend to be higher in quality and impact than the journals protected by the big deals (more in #11 below).

To top it off, most big deals include confidentiality clauses preventing universities from disclosing the prices they pay. The effect is to reduce bargaining and price competition even further. In 2009, three academics launched the Big Deal Contract Project to use state open-record laws to force disclosure of big-deal contracts with public universities. Elsevier went to court to block the release of its contract with Washington State University and lost.[9]

5. During the decades in which journal prices have been rising faster than inflation and faster than library budgets, libraries have cut into their book budgets to pay for journals. According to James McPherson, "In 1986 [academic] libraries spent 44 percent of their budgets on books and 56 percent on journals; by 1997 the imbalance had grown to 28 percent for books and 72 percent for journals." Because academic libraries now buy fewer books, academic book publishers now accept fewer manuscripts. One result is that the journal crisis, concentrated in the sciences, has precipitated a monograph crisis, concentrated in the humanities.[10]

6. New restrictions on electronic journals add a permissions crisis on top of the pricing crisis. For publishers of online toll-access journals, there are business reasons to limit the freedom of users to copy and redistribute texts, even if that leaves users with fewer rights than they had with print journals. But these business reasons create pernicious consequences for libraries and their patrons.

Among the results: When libraries pay for subscriptions to digital journals, they don't buy or own their own digital copies but merely rent or license them for a period of time. If they cancel a subscription, they could lose access to past issues. They could violate the publishers' copyrights if they make or hold copies for long-term preservation without special permission or payment, shifting the task of preservation more and more to publishers who are not preservation experts and who tend to make preservation decisions with only future market potential in mind. Libraries can't migrate older content, such as journal backfiles, to new media and formats to keep them readable as technology changes, at least not without special permission or risk of liability. Some publishers don't allow libraries to share digital texts by interlibrary loan and instead require them to make printouts, scan the printouts, and lend the scans. Libraries must negotiate for prices and licensing terms, often under nondisclosure agreements, and retain and consult complex licensing agreements that differ from publisher to publisher and year to year. They must police or negotiate access for walk-in patrons, online users off campus, and visiting faculty. They must limit access and usage by password, internet-protocol (IP) address, usage hours, institutional affiliation, physical location, and caps on simultaneous users. They must implement authentication systems and administer proxy servers. They must make fair-use judgment calls, erring on the side of seeking permission or forgoing use. They must explain to patrons that cookies and registration make anonymous inquiry impossible and that some uses allowed by law are not allowed by the technology.

I make this list library-centric rather than user-centric because the pricing crisis has nearly killed off individual subscriptions. Most subscribers to toll-access journals are libraries, and most authorized readers of toll-access journals are library patrons.[11]

In short, conventional publishers regard easy online sharing as a problem while researchers and libraries regard it as a solution. The internet is widening the gap between the interests of conventional publishers and the interests of researchers and research institutions.

Conventional publishers are adapting to the digital age in some respects. They're migrating most print journals to digital formats[12] and even dropping their print editions. They're incorporating hyperlinks, search engines, and alert services. A growing number are digitizing their backfiles and integrating texts with data. But the revolutionary

The deeper problem is that we donate time, labor, and public money to create new knowledge and then hand control over the results to businesses that believe, correctly or incorrectly, that their revenue and survival depend on limiting access to that knowledge.

power to share content without price or permission barriers, to solve the pricing and permission crises at a stroke and liberate research for the benefit of all, is the one innovation they fear most.

7. Conventional publishers acquire their key assets from academics without charge. Authors donate the texts of new articles and the rights to publish them. Editors and referees donate the peer-review judgments to improve and validate their quality.[13] But then conventional publishers charge for access to the resulting articles, with no exception for authors, editors, referees, or their institutions. Publishers argue that they add value to the submitted manuscripts, which is true. But other players in the game, such as authors, editors, and referees, add far more value than publishers. For funded research, the funding agency is another critical player. It too must pay for access to the resulting articles even when the cost of a research project is hundreds of thousands of times greater than the cost of publication. Among these five value-adders—authors, editors, referees, funders, and publishers—publishers add the least value and generally demand the ownership rights.

8. Conventional publishers use a business model that depends on access barriers and creates artificial scarcity. All publishers (conventional and OA) need revenue to cover their costs, but OA publishers use business models that dispense with access barriers and avoid artificial scarcity. Toll-access publishers contend that the OA business

models are inadequate. We can debate that, for example, in light of the evidence that more than 7,500 peer-reviewed OA journals are finding ways to pay their bills, the fact that a growing number of for-profit OA publishers are already showing profits, and the fact that most of the money needed to support OA journals is currently tied up supporting toll-access journals. (See chapter 7 on economics.)

But in the end it doesn't matter whether toll-access publishers are right or wrong to believe that their revenue requires access barriers. The deeper problem is that we donate time, labor, and public money to create new knowledge and then hand control over the results to businesses that believe, correctly or incorrectly, that their revenue and survival depend on limiting access to that knowledge. If toll-access publishers are right that they must erect access barriers to reimburse themselves, then the problem is that we allow them to be the only outlets for most peer-reviewed research. If they're wrong about the need for access barriers, then the problem is that we tolerate their access barriers, even for publicly funded research and gifts from authors who write for impact and not for money.

9. Conventional publishers often criticize OA initiatives for "interfering with the market," but scholarly publishing is permeated by state action, public subsidies, gift culture, and anticompetitive practices.[14] All scholarly journals (toll access and OA) benefit from public subsidies. Most scientific research is funded by public agencies us-

ing public money, conducted and written up by researchers working at public institutions and paid with public money, and then peer-reviewed by faculty at public institutions and paid with public money. Even when researchers and peer reviewers work at private universities, their institutions are subsidized by publicly funded tax exemptions and tax-deductible donations. Most toll-access journal subscriptions are purchased by public institutions and paid with taxpayer money.

Last and not least, publishers exercise their control over research articles through copyright, a temporary government-created monopoly.

10. Every scholarly journal is a natural mini-monopoly in the sense that no other journal publishes the same articles. There's nothing improper about this natural mini-monopoly. It's a side-effect of the desirable fact that journals don't duplicate one another. But it means that toll-access journals compete for authors much more than they compete for subscribers. If you need an article published in a certain journal, then you need access to that journal. This is one reason why free and expensive journals can coexist in the same field, even at the same level of quality. The free journals don't drive the expensive journals out of business or even drive down their prices. By weakening the competition for buyers, however, this natural monopoly weakens the market feedback that would otherwise punish declining quality, declining usage, and rising prices.

11. Laid on top of this natural monopoly are several layers of artificial monopoly. One kind of evidence is that large commercial publishers charge higher prices and raise their prices faster than small, nonprofit publishers. Yet, the scholarly consensus is that quality, impact, and prestige are generally higher at the nonprofit society journals.[15]

12. Large conventional publishers spend some of the money they extract from libraries on marketing and "content protection" measures that benefit publishers far more than users. Indeed, the content protection measures don't benefit users at all and make the texts less useful.[16]

13. Conventional for-profit journals can increase their profit margins by decreasing their rejection rates. Reducing the rejection rate reduces the number of articles a journal must peer review for each article it publishes.[17]

14. Most faculty and researchers are aware of access gaps in their libraries but generally unaware of their causes and unaware that the problems are systemic and worsening. (A common response: My research is very specialized, so naturally my library won't have everything I need.) On the other hand, librarians are acutely aware of library budget crises, high journal prices, hyperinflationary price increases, bundling constraints, publisher profit margins, and the disconnect between prices paid and journal costs, size, usage, impact, and quality. Researcher oblivion to the problems facing libraries adds several new problems to the mix. It means that the players who are most aware of

quality are generally unaware of prices, which Jan Velterop once called the "cat food" model of purchasing. It creates a classic moral hazard in which researchers are shielded from the costs of their preferences and have little incentive to adjust their preferences accordingly. It subtracts one more market signal that might otherwise check high prices and declining quality. And while researchers support OA roughly to the extent that they know about it, and have their own reasons to work for it, their general unawareness of the crisis for libraries adds one more difficulty to the job of recruiting busy and preoccupied researchers to the cause of fixing this broken system.[18]

The fact that there are enough problems to motivate different stakeholders is a kind of good news. If the system were broken for buyers (librarians) but not for users (researchers), or vice versa, that would delay any fix even longer. Or it would create a pernicious trade-off in which any fix would help one group at the expense of the other. But the system is broken for both buyers and users, which makes them natural allies.[19]

15. Finally, even in the absence of perverse journal pricing practices, the subscription or toll-access business model would not scale with the growth of research or the growth of published knowledge. If prices were low today and guaranteed to remain low forever, the total price for the total literature would still be heading toward exponential explosion. This is easiest to see at the mythical University

of Croesus, which can afford 100 percent of the literature today. In that respect, Croesus is far better off than any university in the real world. Let's suppose that journal prices and the Croesus library budget increase at the same rate forever. For simplicity, let's assume that rate is zero. They never grow at all, not even at the rate of inflation. Let's assume that the growth of knowledge means that the journal literature grows by 5 percent a year, a common industry estimate. Croesus can afford full coverage today, but in twenty years it would have to spend 2.7 times more than it spends today for full coverage, in sixty years 18.7 times more, and in a hundred years 131.5 times more. But since Croesus can't spend more than it has, in twenty years the coverage it could afford would drop from 100 percent to 37.7 percent, in sixty years to 5.4 percent, and in a hundred years to less than 1 percent.

We need a system of research dissemination that scales with the growth of research volume. The subscription or toll-access system scales negatively by shrinking the accessible percentage of research as research itself continues to grow.[20]

Money would solve the access crisis if we had enough of it, and if the amount at our disposal grew in proportion to the growing volume and growing prices of the literature. But we don't have nearly enough money, and the money we do have doesn't grow nearly fast enough to keep pace with the volume or prices of the literature.

Toll-access publishers don't benefit from access gaps and have their own reasons to want to close them. But they prefer the unscalable money solution, even if university budgets and national treasuries must be squeezed by law to find the funds. Crispin Davis, then-CEO of Elsevier, once argued that "the government needs to lay down guidelines on the proportion of university funds that should be set aside for the acquisition of books and journals, or even increase funding to ensure that universities can buy all the material they need."[21]

At some point we should trust the math more than special-interest lobbies. Among the many who have done the math, the University of California concluded that the subscription model for research journals is "incontrovertibly unsustainable."[22]

2.2   OA as Seizing Opportunities[23]

Even if we had no pressing problems to solve, we'd want to take full advantage of the unprecedented power of digital technology to share knowledge and accelerate research. But we have both problems and opportunities, and we should acknowledge that. Too much of the OA discussion is grim, utilitarian, and problem-oriented. We should complement it with discussion that is joyful, curious, and opportunity-oriented. Serious problems don't rule out beautiful opportunities, and one of the most beautiful opportunities facing OA is that certain strategic actions will solve serious problems and seize beautiful opportunities at the same time.

Here's a brace of those beautiful opportunities. The internet emerged just as journal subscription prices were reaching unbearable levels. The internet widens distribution and reduces costs at the same time. Digital computers connected to a global network let us make perfect copies of arbitrary files and distribute them to a worldwide audience at zero marginal cost. For 350 years, scholars have willingly, even eagerly, published journal articles without payment, freeing them to consent to OA without losing revenue. Unrestricted access to digital files supports forms of discovery and processing impossible for paper texts and for inaccessible or use-restricted digital texts. OA is already lawful and doesn't require copyright reform. Now that the internet is at our fingertips, OA is within the reach of researchers and research institutions acting alone and needn't wait for publishers, legislation, or markets. Authors, editors, and referees—the whole team that produces peer-reviewed research articles—can provide OA to peer-reviewed research literature and, if necessary, cut recalcitrant publishers out of the loop. For researchers acting on their own, the goal of complete OA is even easier to attain than the goal of affordable journals.

A less obvious but more fundamental opportunity is that knowledge is *nonrivalrous* (to use a term from the economics of property). We can share it without dividing it and consume it without diminishing it. My possession and use of some knowledge doesn't exclude your possession and use of the same knowledge.

A less obvious but more fundamental opportunity is that knowledge is *nonrivalrous* (to use a term from the economics of property). We can share it without dividing it and consume it without diminishing it. My possession and use of some knowledge doesn't exclude your possession and use of the same knowledge. Familiar physical goods like land, food, and machines are all *rivalrous*. To share them, we must take turns or settle for portions. Thomas Jefferson described this situation beautifully in an 1813 letter to Isaac McPherson:

> If nature has made any one thing less susceptible
> than all others of exclusive property, it is the action
> of the thinking power called an idea. . . . Its peculiar
> character . . . is that no one possesses the less,
> because every other possesses the whole of it. He who
> receives an idea from me, receives instruction himself
> without lessening mine; as he who lights his taper at
> mine, receives light without darkening mine.[24]

We seldom think about how metaphysically lucky we are that knowledge is nonrivalrous. We can all know the same ideas, stories, tunes, plans, directions, and words without my knowledge blocking yours or yours blocking mine. We're equally fortunate that speech is nonrivalrous, since it allows us to articulate and share our knowledge without reducing it to a rivalrous commodity.

But for all of human history before the digital age, writing has been rivalrous. Written or recorded knowledge became a material object like stone, clay, skin, or paper, which was necessarily rivalrous. Even when we had the printing press and photocopying machine, allowing us to make many copies at comparatively low cost, each copy was a rivalrous material object. Despite its revolutionary impact, writing was hobbled from birth by this tragic limitation. We could only record nonrivalrous knowledge in a rivalrous form.

Digital writing is the first kind of writing that does not reduce recorded knowledge to a rivalrous object. If we all have the right equipment, then we can all have copies of the same digital text without excluding one another, without multiplying our costs, and without depleting our resources.

I've heard physicists refer to the prospect of room-temperature superconductivity as a "gift of nature." Unfortunately, that is not quite within reach. But the nonrivalrous property of digital information is a gift of nature that we've already grasped and put to work. We only have to stand back a moment to appreciate it. To our ancestors, the prospect of recording knowledge in precise language, symbols, sounds, or images without reducing the record to a rivalrous object would have been magical. But we do it every day now, and it's losing its magic.

The danger is not that we already take this property for granted but that we might stop short and fail to take full advantage of it. It can transform knowledge-sharing if we let it.

We take advantage of this gift when we post valuable work online and permit free access and unrestricted use for every user with an internet connection. But if we charge for access, enforce exclusion, create artificial scarcity, or prohibit essential uses, then we treat the nonrivalrous digital file like a rivalrous physical object, dismiss the opportunity, and spurn the gift.

When publishers argue that there is no access problem and that we shouldn't fix what isn't broken, there are two answers. First, they're wrong. There are deep and serious access problems. Publishers who really don't know this should talk to the libraries who subscribe to their journals, and even more to the libraries who don't. But second, leaving that quarrel entirely to one side, there are good reasons to pursue OA anyway.[25]

VARIETIES

There are many ways to deliver OA: personal web sites, blogs, wikis, databases, ebooks, videos, audios, webcasts, discussion forums, RSS feeds, and P2P networks.[1] Unless creative thinking stops now, there will be many more to come.

However, two delivery vehicles dominate the current discussion: journals and repositories.

OA journals are like non-OA journals except that they're OA. Making good on that exception requires a new funding model, but nearly everything else about the journal could be held constant, if we wanted to hold it constant. Some OA journals are very traditional except that they're OA, while others deliberately push the evolution of journals as a category. (Some toll-access journals also push that evolution, if we don't count stopping short of OA.)

Like conventional, toll-access journals, some OA journals are first-rate and some are bottom feeders. Like conventional journals, some OA journals are high in prestige and some are unknown, and some of the unknowns are high in quality and some are low. Some are on solid financial footing and some are struggling. Also like conventional journals, most are honest and some are scams.

As early as 2004, Thomson Scientific found that "in each of the broad subject areas studied there was at least one OA title that ranked at or near the top of its field" in citation impact. The number of high-quality, high-impact OA journals has only grown since.[2]

Unlike toll-access journals, however, most OA journals are new. It's hard to generalize about OA journals beyond saying that they have all the advantages of being OA and all the disadvantages of being new.[3] To be more precise: A disappointing number of OA journals don't have all the advantages of being OA because they retain needless permission barriers. (See section 3.3 on gratis and libre OA.) At the same time, a heartening number of OA journals no longer suffer from the disadvantages of being new.

Like conventional journal publishers, some OA journal publishers are for-profit and some are nonprofit. Like conventional publishers, there are a few large OA publishers and a long tail of small ones, although the largest OA publishers are small compared to the largest conventional publishers. Unlike conventional publishers, the profitable for-profit OA publishers have moderate rather than obscene profit margins.

OA journals and repositories differ in their relationship to peer review. OA journals perform their own peer review, just like conventional journals. Repositories generally don't perform peer review, although they host and disseminate articles peer-reviewed elsewhere. As a result, gold and green OA differ in their support costs and in the roles they can play in the scholarly communications universe.

OA repositories are online collections or databases of articles. Unlike OA journals, OA repositories have no counterpart in the traditional landscape of scholarly communication. That makes them woefully easy to overlook or misunderstand.

By default, new deposits in OA repositories are OA. But most repositories today support *dark deposits*, which can be switched to OA at a later date. Most OA repositories were launched to host peer-reviewed research articles and their preprints. But often they include other sorts of content as well, such as theses and dissertations, datasets, courseware, and digitized copies of works from the special collections of the hosting institution's library. For scholars, repositories are better at making work OA than personal web sites because repositories provide persistent URLs, take steps for long-term preservation, and don't disappear when the author changes jobs or dies.

3.1 Green and Gold OA

Gold and green OA differ in at least two fundamental respects.

First, OA journals and repositories differ in their relationship to peer review. OA journals perform their own peer review, just like conventional journals. Repositories generally don't perform peer review, although they host

> **Terminology**
>
> The OA movement uses the term *gold OA* for OA
> delivered by journals, regardless of the journal's
> business model, and *green OA* for OA delivered
> by repositories. *Self-archiving* is the practice of
> depositing one's own work in an OA repository.
> All three of these terms were coined by Stevan
> Harnad.

and disseminate articles peer-reviewed elsewhere. As a result, gold and green OA differ in their support costs and in the roles they can play in the scholarly communications universe.

Second, OA journals obtain the rights or permissions they need directly from the rightsholders, while repositories ask depositors to obtain the needed rights or permissions on their own. Even when the depositors are the authors themselves, they may already have transferred key rights to publishers. As a result, OA journals can generate permission for reuse at will, and OA repositories generally cannot. Hence, most libre OA is gold OA, even if it's not yet the case that most gold OA is libre OA. (See more in section 3.3 on gratis and libre OA.)

Gold and green OA require different steps from authors. To make new articles gold OA, authors simply submit their manuscripts to OA journals, as they would to conventional journals. To make articles green OA, authors simply deposit their manuscripts in an OA repository.

Most importantly, the green/gold distinction matters because if authors can't make their work OA one way, they can make it OA the other way. One of the most persistent and damaging misunderstandings is that all OA is gold OA. Authors who can't find a high-quality, high-prestige OA journal in their field, or whose submissions are rejected from first-rate OA journals, often conclude that they must give up on OA or publish in a second-rate journal. But that's hasty. If they publish in the best toll-access journal that will accept their work, then—more often than not—they may turn around and deposit the peer-reviewed manuscript in an OA repository. Most toll-access publishers and toll-access journals give blanket permission for green OA, many others will give permission on request, and the numbers approach 100 percent when authors are subject to green OA mandates from their funding agencies or universities. (More in chapters 4 on OA policies and 10 on making your own work OA.)[4]

One of the early victories of the OA movement was to get a majority of toll-access publishers and journals to give blanket permission for author-initiated green OA. But this victory remains one of the best-kept secrets of scholarly publishing, and widespread ignorance of it is the single most harmful consequence of green OA's invisibility. Overlooking this victory reduces the volume of OA and creates the false impression that a trade-off between prestige and OA is common when in fact it is rare. Forgetting that green OA is compatible with conventional publishing also feeds the false impression that policies requiring green OA actually require gold OA and thereby limit the freedom of authors to submit work to the journals of their choice. (More in chapter 4 on policies.)

Most publishing scholars will choose prestige over OA if they have to choose. The good news is that they rarely have to choose. The bad news is that few of them know that they rarely have to choose. Few realize that most toll-access journals permit author-initiated green OA, despite determined efforts to explain and publicize this early victory for green OA.

There are two reasons why OA is compatible with prestigious publication, a gold reason and a green one. The gold reason is that a growing number of OA journals have already earned high levels of prestige, and others are steadily earning it. If there are no prestigious OA journals in your field today, you could wait (things are changing fast), you could help out (by submitting your best work), or you could move on to green. The green reason why OA is compatible with prestige is that most toll-access journals, including the prestigious, already allow OA archiving. As noted, this "most" can become "all" with the aid of an effective OA policy. (See chapter 4 on policies.)

The most useful OA repositories comply with the Open Archives Initiative (OAI) Protocol for Metadata Harvesting (PMH), which makes separate repositories play well together. In the jargon, OAI compliance makes repositories *interoperable*, allowing the worldwide network of individual repositories to behave like a single grand virtual repository that can be searched all at once. It means that users can find a work in an OAI-compliant repository without knowing which repositories exist, where they are located, or what they contain. (OA and OAI are separate but overlapping initiatives.)[5]

Most of the major academic and nonacademic search engines crawl OA journals and OA repositories. For example, Google, Bing, and Yahoo all do this and do it from self-interest. These search engines now provide another method (beyond OAI-based interoperability) for searching across the whole network of repositories without knowing what exists where. A common misunderstanding sees OA repositories as walled gardens that make work hard to find by requiring readers to make separate visits to separate repositories to run separate searches. The reverse is true in two senses: OA repositories make work easier to find, and toll-access collections are the ones more likely to be walled gardens, either invisible to search engines or requiring separate visits and separate searches.

Disciplinary repositories (also called *subject* repositories) try to capture all the research in a given field, while *institutional* repositories try to capture all the research from a given institution. Because both kinds tend to be OAI-compliant and interoperable, the differences matter very little for readers. Readers who want to browse a repository for serendipity are more likely to find useful content in a disciplinary repository in the right field than in an institutional repository. But most scholars find repository content by keyword searches, not by browsing, and through cross-archive searches, not through local single-repository searches.[6]

However, the differences between disciplinary and institutional repositories matter more for authors. On the one hand, institutions are in a better position than disciplines to offer incentives and assistance for deposit, and to adopt policies to ensure deposit. A growing number of universities do just that. On the other hand, scholars who regularly read research in a large disciplinary repository, such as arXiv for physics or PubMed Central for medicine, readily grasp the rationale for depositing their work in OA repositories and need less nudging to do so themselves. (More in chapter 4 on policies.)[7]

Because most publishers and journals already give blanket permission for green OA, the burden is on authors to take advantage of it. In the absence of an institutional policy to encourage or require deposits, the spontaneous rate of deposit is about 15 percent. Institutions requiring deposit can push the rate toward 100 percent over a few years.[8]

The reason the spontaneous rate is lower than the nudged, assisted, and mandated rate is rarely opposition to OA itself. Almost always it's unfamiliarity with green OA (belief that all OA is gold OA), misunderstanding of green OA (belief that it violates copyright, bypasses peer review, or forecloses the possibility of publishing in a venerable journal), and fear that it is time-consuming. In this sense, author unfamiliarity and misunderstanding are greater obstacles to OA than actual opposition, whether from authors or publishers.[9]

The remedies are already spreading worldwide: launching more OA journals and repositories, educating researchers about their gold and green OA options, and adopting intelligent policies to encourage gold OA and require green OA. (More in chapter 4 on OA policies.)

3.2   Green and Gold as Complementary[10]

Some friends of OA focus their energy on green OA and some focus on gold OA. Some support both kinds about equally and have merely specialized. But some give one a higher strategic priority than the other. I'll argue that green and gold OA are complementary and synergistic. We should pursue them simultaneously, much as an organism must develop its nervous system and digestive system simultaneously.

Fortunately, this synergy is served even by differences of opinion about its existence. The fact that some activists give green OA a higher priority than gold, and some the reverse, creates a natural division of labor ensuring that good people are working hard on each front.

Green OA has some advantages over gold OA. It makes faster progress, since it doesn't require the launch of new peer-reviewed journals or the conversion of old ones. For the same reason, it's less expensive than gold OA and can scale up quickly and inexpensively to meet demand, while the bulk of the money needed to scale up OA journals is still tied up in subscriptions to toll-access journals.

Green OA can be mandated without infringing academic freedom, but gold OA cannot. (More precisely, gold OA can't be mandated without infringing academic freedom until virtually all peer-reviewed journals are OA, which isn't on the horizon.) A green OA policy at a university can cover the institution's entire research output, regardless of where authors choose to publish, while a gold OA policy can only cover the new articles that faculty are willing to submit to OA journals.

Green OA is compatible with toll-access publication. Sometimes this is because toll-access publishers hold the needed rights and decide to allow it, and sometimes because authors retain the needed rights. Well-drafted OA policies can ensure that authors always retain the needed rights and spare them the need to negotiate with publishers. (See chapters 4 on policies and 6 on copyright.)

When the best journals in a field are toll-access—often the case today even if changing—green OA allows authors to have their cake and eat it too. Authors good enough to publish in the best journals may do so and still make their work OA, without waiting for high-prestige OA journals to emerge in their fields. When promotion and tenure committees create strong incentives to publish in venerable toll-access journals—often the case today even if changing—green OA allows authors to make their work OA without bucking institutional incentives or relinquishing institutional rewards.

Green OA works for preprints as well as postprints, while gold OA only works for postprints. For the same reason, green OA works for other kinds of work that peer-reviewed journals generally don't publish, such as datasets, source code, theses and dissertations, and digitized copies of work previously available only in another medium such as print, microfiche, or film.

On the other side, gold OA has some advantages over green OA. Gold OA articles needn't labor under restrictions imposed by toll-access publishers fearful of OA. Hence, gold OA is always immediate, while green OA is sometimes embargoed or delayed. Similarly, gold OA can

When the best journals in a field are toll-access—often the case today even if changing—green OA allows authors to have their cake and eat it too. Authors good enough to publish in the best journals may do so and still make their work OA, without waiting for high-prestige OA journals to emerge in their fields.

always be libre, even if it doesn't take sufficient advantage of this opportunity, while green OA seldom even has the opportunity. (See chapter 4 on policies.)

Gold OA provides OA to the published version, while green OA is often limited to the final version of the author's peer-reviewed manuscript, without copy editing or final pagination. Making the OA edition the same as the published edition reduces the confusion caused by the circulation of multiple versions.

Gold OA performs its own peer review, without depending on toll-access journals to perform it. Hence support for gold OA supports the survival of peer review itself in case toll-access journals can no longer provide it.

Finally, green OA may be a manageable expense, but gold OA can be self-sustaining, even profitable.

Librarians traditionally distinguish four functions performed by scholarly journals: Registration (time stamp), certification (peer review), awareness (distribution), and archiving (preservation). We know that green and gold OA are complementary as soon as we recognize that green is better than gold for registration (its time stamps are faster) and preservation, and that gold OA is better than green OA for certification (peer review).

Some see green OA mainly as a tool to force a transition to gold OA. The idea is that rising levels of green OA will trigger the cancellation of conventional journals and pressure them to convert to gold OA. The growing volume of green OA might have this effect. Some publishers fear that it will, and some OA activists hope that it will. But it might not have this effect at all. One piece of evidence is that green OA hasn't triggered journal cancellations in physics, where levels of green OA approach 100 percent and have been high and growing for nearly two decades. (More in chapter 8 on casualties.) Even if it did have this effect, however, it wouldn't follow that it is the best strategy for advancing gold OA. There are good prospects for a peaceful revolution based on publisher consent and self-interest. (More in chapter 7 on economics.)

Most importantly, however, we'll still want green OA in a world where all peer-reviewed journals are OA. For example, we'll want green OA for preprints and for the earliest possible time-stamp to establish the author's priority. We'll want green OA for datasets, theses and dissertations, and other research genres not published in journals. We'll want green OA for the security of having multiple OA copies in multiple independent locations. (Even today, the best OA journals not only distribute their articles from their own web sites but also deposit copies in independent OA repositories.) At least until the very last conventional journal converts to OA, we'll need green OA so that research institutions can mandate OA without limiting the freedom of authors to submit to the journals of their choice. We'll even want OA repositories as the distribution mechanism for many OA journals themselves.

A worldwide network of OA repositories would support one desirable evolution of what we now call journals. It would allow us to decouple peer review from distribution. Peer review could be performed by freestanding editorial boards and distribution by the network of repositories. Decoupling would remove the perverse incentive for peer-review providers to raise access barriers or impede distribution. It would also remove their perverse incentive to demand exclusive rights over research they didn't fund, perform, write up, or buy from the authors.[11]

On the other side, we'll still want gold OA in a world where all new articles are green OA. High-volume green OA may not have caused toll-access journal cancellations yet, even in fields where green OA approaches 100 percent. But we can't say that it will never do so, and we can't say that every field will behave like physics in this respect. If peer-reviewed toll-access journals are not sustainable (see section 2.1), then the survival of peer review will depend on a shift to peer-reviewed OA journals.

It won't matter whether toll-access journals are endangered by rising levels of green OA, by their own hyperinflationary price increases, or by their failure to scale with the rapid growth of new research. If any combination of these causes puts peer-reviewed toll-access journals in jeopardy, then peer review will depend on OA journals, which are not endangered by any of those causes. (In chapter 8 on casualties, we'll see evidence that toll-access journal price increases cause many more cancellations than green OA does.)

Finally, if all new articles are green OA, we'll still want the advantages that are easier for gold OA than for green OA to provide: freedom from permission barriers, freedom from delays or embargoes, and freedom from ever-rising drains on library budgets.

Neither green nor gold OA will suffice, long-term or short-term. That's a reason to pursue both.

3.3 Gratis and Libre OA[12]

Sometimes we must speak unambiguously about two subspecies of OA. One removes price barriers alone and the other removes price barriers and at least some permission barriers. The former is *gratis OA* and the latter *libre OA*.

To sharpen their definitions, we need a quick detour into fair use. In the United States, fair use is an exception to copyright law allowing users to reproduce copyrighted work "for purposes such as criticism, comment, news reporting, teaching . . . , scholarship, or research" (to quote the U.S. copyright statute).[13]

Fair use has four characteristics that matter to us here. First, the permission for fair use is granted by law and needn't be sought from the copyright holder. Or equivalently, the statute assures us that no permission is needed because fair use "is not an infringement of copyright." Second, the permission is limited and doesn't cover all the uses that scholars might want to make. To exceed fair use, users must obtain permission from the copyright holder. Third, most countries have some equivalent of fair use, though they differ significantly in what they allow and disallow. Finally, fair use is vague. There are clear cases of fair use (quoting a short snippet in a review) and clear cases of exceeding fair use (reprinting a full-text book), but the boundary between the two is fuzzy and contestable.

Gratis OA is free of charge but not more free than that. Users must still seek permission to exceed fair use. Gratis OA removes price barriers but not permission barriers.

Libre OA is free of charge and also free of some copyright and licensing restrictions. Users have permission to exceed fair use, at least in certain ways. Because there are many ways to exceed fair use, there are many degrees or kinds of libre OA. Libre OA removes price barriers and at least some permission barriers.

Fortunately, we don't always need these terms. Indeed, in most of this book I use "OA" without qualification. The generic term causes no trouble until we need to talk about differences between gratis and libre OA, just as "carbohydrate" causes no trouble until we need to talk about differences between simple and complex carbohydrates.

I'm borrowing the gratis/libre language from the world of software, where it expresses the same distinction. If the terms sound odd in English, it's because English doesn't have more domesticated terms for this distinction. Their oddity in English may even be an advantage, since the terms don't carry extra baggage, as "open" and "free" do, which therefore helps us avoid ambiguity.[14]

First note that the gratis/libre distinction is not the same as the green/gold distinction. The gratis/libre distinction is about user rights or freedoms, while the green/gold distinction is about venues or vehicles. Gratis/libre answers the question, *how open is it?* Green/gold answers the question, *how is it delivered?*[15]

Green OA can be gratis or libre but is usually gratis. Gold OA can be gratis or libre, but is also usually gratis. However, it's easier for gold OA to be libre than for green OA to be libre, which is why the campaign to go beyond gratis OA to libre OA focuses more on journals than repositories.

If users encounter a full-text work online without charge, then they know it's gratis OA. They don't have to be told, even if they'd like to be told—for example, so that they don't have to wonder whether they're reading an illicit copy. But users can't figure out whether a work is libre OA unless the provider (author or publisher) tells them. This is the purpose of a *license*, which is simply a statement from the copyright holder explaining what users may and may not do with a given work.

Works under "all-rights-reserved" copyrights don't need licenses, because "all rights reserved" means that without special permission users may do nothing that exceeds fair use.

The default around the world today is that new works are copyrighted from birth (no registration required), that the copyright initially belongs to the author (but is transferrable by contract), and that the rights holder reserves all rights. Authors who want to provide libre OA must affirmatively waive some of their rights and use a license to tell users they've done so. For convenience, let's say that an *open license* is one allowing some degree of libre OA.

Although the word "copyright" is singular, it covers a plurality of rights, and authors may waive some and retain others. They may do so in any combination that suits their needs. That's why there are many nonequivalent open licenses and nonequivalent types of libre OA. What's important here is that waiving some rights in order to provide libre OA does not require waiving all rights or waiving copyright altogether. On the contrary, open licenses presuppose copyright, since they express permissions from the copyright holder. Moreover, the rights not waived are fully enforceable. In the clear and sensible language of Creative Commons, open licenses create "some-rights-reserved" copyrights rather than "all-rights-reserved" copyrights.

The open licenses from Creative Commons (CC) are the best-known and most widely used. But there are other open licenses, and authors and publishers can always write their own. To illustrate the range of libre OA, however, it's convenient to look at the CC licenses.[16]

The maximal degree of libre OA belongs to works in the public domain. Either these works were never under copyright or their copyrights have expired. Works in the public domain may be used in any way whatsoever without violating copyright law. That's why it's lawful to translate or reprint Shakespeare without hunting down his heirs for permission. Creative Commons offers CC0 (CC-Zero) for copyright holders who want to assign their work to the public domain.[17]

The CC Attribution license (CC-BY) describes the least restrictive sort of libre OA after the public domain. It allows any use, provided the user attributes the work to the original author. This is the license recommended by the Open Access Scholarly Publishers Association (OASPA) and the SPARC Europe Seal of Approval program for OA journals.[18] I support this recommendation, use CC-BY for my blog and newsletter, and request CC-BY whenever I publish in a journal.

CC supports several other open licenses as well, including CC-BY-NC, which requires attribution and blocks commercial use, and CC-BY-ND, which requires attribution and allows commercial use but blocks derivative works. These licenses are not equivalent to one another, but they all permit uses beyond fair use and therefore they all represent different flavors of libre OA.

While you can write your own open licenses or use those created by others, the advantage of CC licenses is that they are ready-made, lawyer-drafted, enforceable, understood by a large and growing number of users, and available in a large and growing number of legal jurisdictions. Moreover, each comes in three versions: human-readable for nonlawyers, lawyer-readable for lawyers and judges, and machine-readable for search engines and other visiting software. They're extremely convenient and their convenience has revolutionized libre OA.

The best way to refer to a specific flavor of libre OA is by referring to a specific open license. We'll never have unambiguous, widely understood technical terms for every useful variation on the theme. But we already have clearly named licenses for all the major variations on the theme, and we can add new ones for more subtle variations any time we want.

A work without an open license stands or appears to stand under an all-rights-reserved copyright. If the rights holder privately welcomes uses beyond fair use, or has decided not to sue for certain kinds of infringement, ordinary users have no way to know that and are forced to choose the least of three evils: the delay of asking permission, the risk of proceeding without it, and the harm of erring on the side of nonuse. These are not only obstacles to research; they are obstacles that libre OA was designed to remove.

The BBB definition calls for both gratis and libre OA. However, most of the notable OA success stories are gratis and not libre. I mean this in two senses: gratis success stories are more numerous than libre success stories, so far, and most gratis success stories are notable. Even if they stop short of libre OA, they are hard-won victories and major advances.

Some observers look at the prominent gratis OA success stories and conclude that the OA movement focuses on gratis OA and neglects libre. Others look at the public definitions and conclude that OA focuses on libre OA and disparages gratis. Both assessments are one-sided and unfair.

One hard fact is that gratis OA is often attainable in circumstances when libre OA is not attainable. For example, a major victory of the OA movement has been to persuade the majority of toll-access publishers and toll-access journals to allow green gratis OA. We're very far from the same position for green libre OA. Similarly, most of the strong OA policies at funding agencies and universities require green gratis OA. A few require green libre OA, and green libre OA is growing for other reasons. But if these funders and universities had waited until they could muster the votes for a green libre policy, most of them would still be waiting. (See section 4.3 on the historical timing of OA policies.)

A second hard fact is that even gratis OA policies can face serious political obstacles. They may be easier to adopt than libre policies, but in most cases they're far from easy. The OA policy at the U.S. National Institutes of Health was first proposed by Congress in 2004, adopted as a mere request or encouragement in 2005, and strengthened into a requirement in 2008. Every step along the way was strenuously opposed by an aggressive and well-funded publishing lobby. Yet even now the policy provides only gratis OA, not libre OA. Similarly, the gratis OA policies at funders and universities were only adopted after years of patiently educating decision-makers and answering their objections and misunderstandings. Reaching the point of adoption, and especially unanimous votes for adoption, is a cause for celebration, even if the policies only provide gratis, not libre OA.[19]

The Directory of Open Access Journals is the most authoritative catalog of OA journals and the only one limiting itself to peer-reviewed journals. But only 20 percent of titles in the DOAJ use CC licenses, and fewer than 11 percent use the recommended CC-BY license. Viewed the other way around, about 80 percent of peer-reviewed OA journals don't use any kind of CC license. Some of these might use non-CC licenses with a similar legal effect, but these exceptions are rare. Simply put, most OA journals are not using open licenses. Most operate under all-rights-reserved copyrights and leave their users with no more freedom than they already had under fair use. Most are not offering libre OA. Even those wanting to block commercial use, for example, tend to use an all-rights-reserved copyright rather than an open license that blocks commercial use, such as CC-BY-NC, but allows libre OA in other respects.[20]

I've argued that it's unfair to criticize the OA movement for disparaging gratis OA (merely on the ground that its public statements call for libre) or neglecting libre OA (merely on the ground that most of its success stories are gratis). But two related criticisms would be more just. First, demanding libre or nothing where libre is currently unattainable makes the perfect the enemy of the good. Fortunately, this tactical mistake is rare. Second, settling for gratis where libre is attainable makes the good a substitute for the better. Unfortunately, this tactical mistake is common, as we see from the majority of OA journals that stop at gratis when they could easily offer libre.

Let's be more specific about the desirability of libre OA. Why should we bother, especially when we may already have attained gratis OA? The answer is that we need libre OA to spare users the delay and expense of seeking permission whenever they want to exceed fair use. And there are good scholarly reasons to exceed fair use. For example:

- to quote long excerpts

- to distribute full-text copies to students or colleagues

- to burn copies on CDs for bandwidth-poor parts of the world

- to distribute semantically-tagged or otherwise enhanced (i.e., modified) versions

- to migrate texts to new formats or media to keep them readable as technologies change

- to create and archive copies for long-term preservation

- to include works in a database or mashup

- to make an audio recording of a text

- to translate a text into another language

- to copy a text for indexing, text-mining, or other kinds of processing

In some jurisdictions, some of these uses may actually fall under fair use, even if most do not. Courts have settled some of the boundaries of fair use but by no means all of them, and in any case users can't be expected to know all the relevant court rulings. Uncertainty about these boundaries, and increasingly severe penalties for copyright infringement, make users fear liability and act cautiously. It makes them decide that they can't use something they'd like to use, or that they must delay their research in order to seek permission.

Libre OA under open licenses solves all these problems. Even when a desirable use is already allowed by fair use, a clear open license removes all doubt. When a desirable use does exceed fair use, a clear open license removes the restriction and offers libre OA.

When you can offer libre OA, don't leave users with no more freedom than fair use. Don't leave them uncertain about what they may and may not do. Don't make conscientious users choose between the delay of seeking permission and the risk of proceeding without it. Don't increase the pressure to make users less conscientious. Don't make them pay for permission. Don't make them err on the side of nonuse. Make your work as usable and useful as it can possibly be.[21]

POLICIES

4.1 OA Policies at Funding Agencies and Universities[1]

Authors control the volume and growth of OA. They decide whether to submit their work to OA journals (gold OA), whether to deposit their work in OA repositories (green OA), and how to use their copyrights. But scholarly authors are still largely unfamiliar with their OA options. It's pointless to appeal to them as a bloc because they don't act as a bloc. It's not hard to persuade or even excite them once we catch their attention, but because they are so anarchical, overworked, and preoccupied, it's hard to catch their attention.

Fortunately, funding agencies and universities are discovering their own interests in fostering OA. These nonprofit institutions make it their mission to advance research and to make that research as useful and widely available as possible. Their money frees researchers to do their work and avoid the need to tie their income to the popularity of their ideas. Above all, these institutions are in an unparalleled position to influence author decisions.

Today, more than fifty funding agencies and more than one hundred universities have adopted strong OA policies. Each one depends on the primacy of author decisions.[2]

One kind of policy, better than nothing, requests or encourages OA. A stronger kind of policy requires OA or makes it the default for new work. These stronger policies are usually called OA *mandates* and I'll use that term for lack of a better one (but see section 4.2 on how it's misleading).

0. *Request or encouragement policies*   These merely ask faculty to make their work OA, or recommend OA for their new work. Sometimes they're called resolutions or pledges rather than policies.[3]

Encouragement policies can target green and gold OA equally. By contrast, mandates only make sense for green OA, at least today when OA journals constitute only about one-quarter of peer-reviewed journals. A gold OA mandate would put most peer-reviewed journals off-limits and seriously limit faculty freedom to submit their work to the journals of their choice. This problem doesn't arise for green OA mandates.

Fortunately, this is well understood. There are no gold OA mandates anywhere; all OA mandates are green. Unfortunately, however, many people mistakenly believe that all OA is gold OA and therefore mistake proposed green OA mandates for proposed gold OA mandates and raise objections that would only apply to gold OA mandates. But as more academics understand the green/gold distinction, and understand that well-written green OA mandates are compatible with academic freedom, more institutions are adopting green OA mandates, almost always at the initiative of faculty themselves.[4]

At universities, there are roughly three approaches to green OA mandates:

1. *Loophole mandates*   These require green OA except when the author's publisher doesn't allow it.[5]

2. *Deposit mandates*   These require deposit in an OA repository as soon as the article is accepted for publication, but they separate the timing of deposit from the timing of OA. If the author's publisher doesn't allow OA, then these policies keep the deposited article dark or non-OA. If the publisher allows OA, immediately or after some embargo, then the deposit becomes OA as soon as the permission kicks in. Because most publishers allow OA on some timetable, this method will provide OA to most new work in due time.

Deposit mandates generally depend on publisher permission for OA, just like loophole mandates. The difference is that they require deposit even when they can't obtain permission for OA.[6]

3. *Rights-retention mandates*   These require deposit in an OA repository as soon as the article is accepted for publication, just like deposit mandates. But they add a method to secure permission for making the deposit OA. There's more than one way to secure that permission. At the Wellcome Trust and NIH, which pioneered this approach for funding agencies, when grantees publish articles based on their funded research they must retain the nonexclusive right to authorize OA through a repository. At Harvard, which pioneered this approach for universities, faculty members vote to give the university a standing nonexclusive right (among other nonexclusive rights) to make their future work OA through the institutional repository. When faculty publish articles after that, the university already has the needed permission, and faculty needn't take any special steps to retain rights or negotiate with publishers. Nor need they wait for the publisher's embargo to run. Harvard-style policies also give faculty a waiver option, allowing them to opt out of the grant of permission to the university, though not out of the deposit requirement. When faculty members obtain waivers for given works, then Harvard-style mandates operate like deposit

mandates and the works remain dark deposits until the institution has permission to make them OA.[7]

Many OA policies are crossbreeds rather than pure types, but all the policies I've seen are variations on these four themes.

First note that none of the three "mandates" absolutely requires OA. Loophole mandates allow some work to escape through the loophole. Deposit mandates allow some deposited work to remain dark (non-OA), by following publisher preferences. Rights-retention mandates with waiver options allow some work to remain dark, by following author preferences.

Loophole and deposit policies defer to publishers for permissions, while rights-retention policies obtain permission from authors before they transfer rights to publishers. For loophole and deposit policies, permission is contingent, because some publishers are willing and some are not. For rights-retention policies, permission is assured, at least initially or by default, although authors may opt out for any publication.

When loophole policies can't provide OA, covered works needn't make it to the repository even as dark deposits. When deposit and rights-retention policies can't provide OA, at least they require dark deposit for the texts, and OA for the metadata (information about author, title, date, and so on). Releasing the metadata makes even a dark deposit visible to readers and search engines. Moreover, many repositories support an email-request button for works on dark deposit. The button enables a reader to submit a one-click request for a full-text email copy and enables the author to grant or deny the request with a one-click response.[8]

We could say that rights-retention policies require OA except when authors opt out, or that they simply shift the default to OA. Those are two ways of saying the same thing because, either way, faculty remain free to decide for or against OA for each of their publications. Preserving this freedom and making it conspicuous help muster faculty support, indeed, unanimous faculty votes. Because shifting the default is enough to change behavior on a large scale, waiver options don't significantly reduce the volume of OA. At Harvard the waiver rate is less than 5 percent, and at MIT it's less than 2 percent.

Loophole policies and rights-retention policies both offer opt-outs. But loophole policies give the opt-out to publishers and rights-retention policies give it to authors. The difference is significant because many more authors than publishers want OA for research articles.

Many institutions adopt loophole policies because they believe a blanket exemption for dissenting publishers is the only way to avoid copyright problems. But that is not true. Deposit policies don't make works OA until publishers allow OA, and rights-retention policies close the loophole and obtain permission directly from authors at a time when authors are the copyright holders.

OA policies from funding agencies are very much like OA policies from universities. They can encourage green and gold OA, or they can require green OA. If they require green OA, they can do so in one of the three ways above. If there's a difference, it's that when funders adopt a rights-retention mandate, they typically don't offer waiver options. On the contrary, the Wellcome Trust and NIH require their grantees to make their work OA through a certain OA repository on a certain timetable and to retain the right to authorize that OA. If a given publisher will not allow grantees to comply with their prior funding agreement, then grantees must look for another publisher.[9]

There are two reasons why these strong funder policies don't infringe faculty freedom to submit work to their journals of their choice. First, researchers needn't seek funds from these funders. When they choose to do so, then they agree to the OA provisions, just as they agree to the other terms and conditions of the grant. The OA "mandate" is a condition on a voluntary contract, not an unconditional requirement. It's a reasonable condition as well, since public funders, like the NIH, disburse public money in the public interest, and private funders, like the Wellcome Trust, disburse charitable money for charitable purposes. To my knowledge, no researchers have refused to apply for Wellcome or NIH funds because of the OA condition, even when they plan to publish in OA-averse journals. The OA condition benefits authors and has not been a deal-breaker.

Second, virtually all publishers accommodate these policies. For example, no surveyed publishers anywhere refuse to publish work by NIH-funded authors on account of the agency's OA mandate. Hence, in practice grantees may still submit work to the journals of their choice, even without a waiver option to accommodate holdout publishers.[10]

We should never forget that most toll-access journals already allow green OA and that a growing number of high-quality, high-prestige peer-reviewed journals are gold OA. From one point of view, we don't need OA mandates when authors already plan to publish in one of those journals. But sometimes toll-access journals change their positions on green OA. Sometimes authors don't get around to making their work green OA even when their journals allow it. And sometimes authors don't publish in one of those journals. The final rationale for green OA mandates, then, is for institutions to bring about OA for their entire research output, regardless of how publishers might alter their policies, regardless of author inertia, and regardless of the journals in which faculty or grantees choose to publish.

Green OA mandates don't assure OA to the entire research output of a university or funding agency, for the same reason that they don't require OA without

The OA "mandate" is a condition on a voluntary contract, not an unconditional requirement. It's a reasonable condition as well, since public funders, like the NIH, disburse public money in the public interest, and private funders, like the Wellcome Trust, disburse charitable money for charitable purposes.

qualification. But implementing them provides OA to a much larger percentage of the research output than was already headed toward OA journals or OA repositories, and does so while leaving authors free to submit their work to the journals of their choice.

I've only tried to give a rough taxonomy of OA policies and their supporting arguments. For detailed recommendations on OA policy provisions, and specific arguments for them, see my 2009 analysis of policy options for funding agencies and universities.[11]

I've also focused here on OA policies for peer-reviewed research articles. Many universities have adopted OA mandates for theses and dissertations, and many funder OA policies also cover datasets. A growing number of universities supplement OA mandates for articles with a sensible and effective policy to assure compliance: When faculty come up for promotion or tenure, the review committee will only consider journal articles on deposit in the institutional repository.[12]

4.2 Digression on the Word "Mandate"[13]

The strongest OA policies use words like "must" or "shall" and require or seem to require OA. They're commonly called OA "mandates." But all three varieties of university "mandate" above show why the term is misleading. Loophole mandates don't require OA without qualification: when publishers dissent, articles are either not deposited in the repository or not made OA. Deposit mandates don't require OA without qualification: when publishers dissent, articles are deposited in a repository but are not made OA. Rights-retention mandates with waiver options don't require OA without qualification: authors may obtain waivers and sometimes do. I haven't seen a university OA "mandate" anywhere without at least one of these three kinds of flexibility.

That's the main reason why no university policies require OA without qualification. There are a few more. First, as Harvard's Stuart Shieber frequently argues, even the strongest university policies can't make tenured faculty comply.[14] Second, as I've frequently argued, successful policies are implemented through expectations, education, incentives, and assistance, not coercion. Third, even the strongest policies—even the no-loophole, no-deference, no-waiver policies at the Wellcome Trust and NIH—make OA a condition on a voluntary contract. No policy anywhere pretends to impose an unconditional OA requirement, and it's hard to imagine how any policy could even try. ("You must make your work OA even if you don't work for us or use our funds"?)

Unfortunately, we don't have a good vocabulary for policies that use mandatory language while deferring to third-person dissents or offering first-person opt-outs.

Nor do we have a good vocabulary for policies that use mandatory language and replace enforcement with compliance-building through expectations, education, incentives, and assistance. The word "mandate" is not a very good fit for policies like this, but neither is any other English word.

By contrast, we do have a good word for policies that use mandatory language for those who agree to be bound. We call them "contracts." While "contract" is short, accurate, and unfrightening, it puts the accent on the author's consent to be bound. That's often illuminating, but just as often we want to put the accent on the content's destiny to become OA. For that purpose, "mandate" has become the term of art, for better or worse.[15]

I use "mandate" with reluctance because it can frighten some of the people I'm trying to persuade and can give rise to misunderstandings about the policies behind the label. When we have time and space for longer phrases, we can talk about "putting an OA condition" on research grants, in the case of NIH-style policies, or "shifting the default to OA" for faculty research, in the case of Harvard-style policies. These longer expressions are more accurate and less frightening. However, sometimes we need a shorthand term, and we need a term that draws an appropriately sharp contrast with policies that merely request or encourage OA.

If anyone objects that a policy containing mandatory language and a waiver option isn't really a "mandate," I won't disagree. On the contrary, I applaud them for recognizing a nuance which too many others overlook. (It's depressing how many PhDs can read a policy with mandatory language and a waiver option, notice the mandatory language, overlook the waiver option, and then cite the lack of flexibility as an objection.) But denying that a policy is a mandate can create its own kinds of misunderstanding. In the United States, citizens called for jury duty must appear, even if many can claim exemptions and go home again. We can say that jury duty with exemptions isn't really a "duty," provided we don't conclude that it's merely a request and encouragement.

Finally, a common misunderstanding deliberately promulgated by some publishers is that OA must be "mandated" because faculty don't want it. This position gets understandable but regrettable mileage from the word "mandate." It also overlooks decisive counter-evidence that we've had in hand since 2004. Alma Swan's empirical studies of researcher attitudes show that an overwhelming majority of researchers would "willingly" comply with a mandatory OA policy from their funder or employer.[16]

The most recent evidence of faculty willingness is the stunning series of strong OA policies adopted by unanimous faculty votes. (When is the last time you heard of a unanimous faculty vote for anything, let alone anything of importance?) As recently as 2007, speculation that we'd soon see more than two dozen unanimous faculty votes for OA policies would have been dismissed as wishful thinking. But now that the evidence lies before us, what looks like wishful thinking is the publishing lobby's idea that OA must be mandated because faculty don't want it.[17]

Finally, the fact that faculty vote unanimously for strong OA policies is a good reason to keep looking for a better word than "mandate." At least it's a good reason to look past the colloquial implications of the term to the policies themselves and the players who drafted and adopted them. Since 2008, most OA "mandates" at universities have been self-imposed by faculty.

4.3   Digression on the Historical Timing of OA Policies[18]

Some kinds of strong OA policy that are politically unattainable or unwise today may become attainable and wise in the future. Here are three examples.

1. Today, a libre green mandate (say, one giving users the right to copy and redistribute, not just access for reading) would face serious publisher resistance. Even if the policy included rights retention and didn't depend on publishers for permissions, publisher resistance would still matter because publishers possess—and ought to

possess—the right to refuse to publish any work for any reason. They could refuse to publish authors bound by a libre green policy, or they could insist on a waiver from the policy as a condition of publication. Policies triggering rejections hurt authors, and policies driving up waiver rates don't do much to help OA. However, publisher resistance might diminish as the ratio of OA publishers to toll-access publishers tilts toward OA, as spontaneous author submissions shift toward OA journals, or as the number of institutions with libre green mandates makes resistance more costly than accommodation for publishers. When OA policies are toothless, few in number, or concentrated in small institutions, then they must accommodate publishers in order to avoid triggering rejections and hurting authors. But as policies grow in number, scope, and strength, the situation could flip over, and publishers will have to accommodate OA policies in order to avoid hurting themselves by rejecting too many good authors for reasons unrelated to the quality of their work.[19]

2. Today, a gold OA mandate would limit faculty freedom to submit work to the journals of their choice. But that's because today only about 25 percent of peer-reviewed journals are OA. As this percentage grows, then a gold OA mandate's encroachment on academic freedom shrinks. At some point even the most zealous defenders of faculty freedom may decide that the encroachment is negligible. In principle the encroachment could be zero,

The moments of opportunity will not be obvious. They . . . will call for some self-fulfilling leadership. Institutional policy-makers will have to assess not only the climate created by existing policies, and existing levels of support, but also the likely effects of their own actions.

though of course when the encroachment is zero, and gold OA mandates are harmless, then gold OA mandates would also be unnecessary.

3. Today, faculty voting for a rights-retention OA mandate want a waiver option, and when the option is available their votes tend to be overwhelming or unanimous. But there are several circumstances that might make it attractive for faculty to abolish waiver options or make waivers harder to obtain. One is a shift in faculty perspective that makes access to research more urgent than indulging publishers who erect access barriers. Another is a significant rise in publisher acceptance of green OA, which gives virtually all authors—rather than just most—blanket permission for green OA. In the first case, faculty might "vote with their submissions" and steer clear of publishers who don't allow author-initiated green OA. In the second case, faculty would virtually never encounter such publishers. In the first case, they'd seldom want waivers, and the second they'd seldom need waivers.

It's understandable that green gratis mandates are spreading faster than green libre mandates, that green mandates in general are spreading faster than gold mandates, and that rights-retention policies with waiver options are spreading faster than rights-retention policies without waivers. However, there is modest growth on one of these fronts: green libre mandates.[20]

The case against these three kinds of OA policy is time-sensitive, not permanent. It's circumstantial, and circumstances are changing. But the strategy for institutions wanting to remove access barriers to research is unchanging: they should adopt the strongest policies they can today and watch for the moment when they could strengthen them.

As researchers become more familiar with OA, as more institutions adopt OA policies, as more new literature is covered by strong OA policies, as more toll-access journals convert to OA, as more toll-access journals accommodate OA mandates without converting, and even as more OA journals shift from gratis to libre, institutions will be able strengthen their OA policies without increasing publisher-controlled rejection rates or author-controlled waiver rates. They should watch the shifting balance of power and seize opportunities to strengthen their policies.

The moments of opportunity will not be obvious. They will not be highlighted by objective evidence alone and will call for some self-fulfilling leadership. Institutional policymakers will have to assess not only the climate created by existing policies, and existing levels of support, but also the likely effects of their own actions. Every strong, new policy increases the likelihood of publisher accommodation, and when enough universities and funders have policies, all publishers will have to accommodate them. In that sense, every strong new policy creates some of the conditions of its own success. Every institution adopting a new policy brings about OA for the research it controls and makes the way easier for other institutions behind it. Like many other policy issues, this is one on which it is easier to follow than to lead, and we already have a growing number of leaders. A critical mass is growing and every policy is an implicit invitation to other institutions to gain strength through common purpose and help accelerate publisher adaptation.

SCOPE

As we saw in chapter 1, any kind of content can in principle be OA. Any kind of content can be digitized, and any kind of digital content can be put online without price or permission barriers. In that sense, the potential scope of OA is universal. Hence, instead of saying that OA applies to some categories or genres and not to others, it's better to say that some categories are easier and some harder.

OA is not limited to the sciences, where it is known best and moving fastest, but extends to the arts and humanities. It's not limited to research created in developed countries, where it is most voluminous, but includes research from developing countries. (Nor, conversely, is it limited to research from developing countries, where the need is most pressing.) It's not limited to publicly funded research, where the argument is almost universally accepted, but includes privately funded and unfunded research. It's not limited to present and future publications, where most policies focus, but includes past publications. It's not limited to born-digital work, where the technical barriers are lowest, but includes work digitized from print, microfiche, film, and other media. It's not limited to text, but includes data, audio, video, multimedia, and executable code.

There are serious, practical, successful campaigns to provide OA to the many kinds of content useful to scholars, including:

- peer-reviewed research articles

- unrefereed preprints destined to be peer-reviewed research articles

- theses and dissertations

- research data

- government data

- source code

- conference presentations (texts, slides, audio, video)

- scholarly monographs

- textbooks

- novels, stories, plays, and poetry

- newspapers

- archival records and manuscripts

- images (artworks, photographs, diagrams, maps)

- teaching and learning materials ("open education resources" and "open courseware")

- digitized print works (some in the public domain, some still under copyright)

For some of these categories, such as data and source code, we need OA to facilitate the testing and replication of scientific experiments. For others, such as data, images, and digitized work from other media, we need OA in order to give readers the same chance to analyze the primary materials that the authors had. For others, such as articles, monographs, dissertations, and conference presentations, we need OA simply to share results and analysis with everyone who might benefit from them.

A larger book could devote sections to each category. Here I focus on just a few.

5.1 Preprints, Postprints, and Peer Review[1]

Throughout most of its history, newcomers to OA assumed that the whole idea was to bypass peer review. That assumption was false and harmful, and we've made good progress in correcting it. The purpose of OA is to remove access barriers, not quality filters. Today many peer-reviewed OA journals are recognized for their excellence, many excellent peer-reviewed toll-access journal publishers are experimenting with OA, and green OA for peer-reviewed articles is growing rapidly. Unfortunately many newcomers unaware of these developments still assume that the purpose of OA is to bypass peer review. Some of them deplore the prospect, some rejoice in it, and their passion spreads the misinformation even farther.

All the public statements in support of OA stress the importance of peer review. Most of the enthusiasm for OA is enthusiasm for OA to peer-reviewed literature. At the same time, we can acknowledge that many of the people working hard for this goal are simultaneously exploring new forms of scholarly communication that exist outside the peer-review system, such as preprint exchanges, blogs, wikis, databases, discussion forums, and social media.

In OA lingo, a "preprint" is any version of an article prior to peer review, such as a draft circulating among colleagues or the version submitted to a journal. A "postprint" is any version approved by peer review. The scope of green OA deliberately extends to both preprints and postprints, just as the function of gold OA deliberately includes peer review.[2]

We could say that OA preprint initiatives focus on bypassing peer review. But it would be more accurate to say

In OA lingo, a "preprint" is any version of an article prior to peer review, such as a draft circulating among colleagues or the version submitted to a journal. A "postprint" is any version approved by peer review.

that they focus on OA for works destined for peer review but not yet peer reviewed. Preprint exchanges didn't arise because they bypass peer review but because they bypass delay. They make new work known more quickly to people in the field, creating new and earlier opportunities for citation, discussion, verification, and collaboration. How quickly? They make new work public the minute that authors are ready to make it public.

OA preprints offer obvious reader-side benefits to those tracking new developments. But this may be a case where the author-side benefits swamp the reader-side benefits. Preprint exchanges give authors the earliest possible time stamp to mark their priority over others working on the same problem. (Historical aside: It's likely that in the seventeenth century, journals superseded books as the primary literature of science precisely because they were faster than books in giving authors an authoritative public time stamp.)

Preprint exchanges existed before the internet, but OA makes them faster, larger, more useful, and more widely read. Despite these advantages, however, preprint exchanges don't represent the whole OA movement or even the whole green OA movement. On the contrary, most green OA and most OA overall focuses on peer-reviewed articles.

As soon as scholars had digital networks to connect peers together, they began using them to tinker with peer review. Can we use networks to find good referees, or to gather, share, and weigh their comments? Can we use networks to implement traditional models of peer review more quickly or effectively? Can we use networks to do better than the traditional models? Many scholars answer "yes" to some or all of these questions, and many of those saying "yes" also support OA. One effect is a creative and long-overdue efflorescence of experiments with new forms of peer review. Another effect, however, is the false perception that OA entails peer-review reform. For example, many people believe that OA requires a certain kind of peer review, favors some kinds of peer review and disfavors others, can't proceed until we agree on the best form of peer review, or benefits only those who support certain kinds of peer-review reforms. All untrue.

OA is compatible with every kind of peer review, from the most traditional and conservative to the most networked and innovative. Some OA journals deliberately adopt traditional models of peer review, in order to tweak just the access variable of scholarly journals. Some deliberately use very new models, in order to push the evolution of peer review. OA is a kind of access, not a kind of editorial policy. It's not intrinsically tied to any particular model of peer review any more than it's intrinsically tied to any particular business model or method of digital preservation.

With one exception, achieving OA and reforming peer review are independent projects. That is, we can achieve

OA without reforming peer review, and we can reform peer review without achieving OA. The exception is that some new forms of peer review presuppose OA.

For example, *open review* makes submissions OA, before or after some prepublication review, and invites community comments. Some open-review journals will use those comments to decide whether to accept the article for formal publication, and others will already have accepted the article and use the community comments to complement or carry forward the quality evaluation started by the journal. Open review requires OA, but OA does not require open review.

Peer review does not depend on the price or medium of a journal. Nor does the value, rigor, or integrity of peer review. We know that peer review at OA journals can be as rigorous and honest as peer review at the best toll-access journals because it can use the same procedures, the same standards, and even the same people (editors and referees) as the best toll-access journals. We see this whenever toll-access journals convert to OA without changing their methods or personnel.

5.2   Theses and Dissertations[3]

Theses and dissertations are the most useful kinds of invisible scholarship and the most invisible kinds of useful scholarship. Because of their high quality and low visibility, the access problem is worth solving.

Fortunately OA for electronic theses and dissertations (ETDs) is easier than for any other kind of research literature. Authors have not yet transferred rights to a publisher, no publisher permissions are needed, no publisher fears need be answered, and no publisher negotiations slow things down or make the outcome uncertain. Virtually all theses and dissertations are now born digital, and institutions expecting electronic submission generally provide OA, the reverse of the default for journal publishers.

The chief obstacle seems to be author fear that making a thesis or dissertation OA will reduce the odds that a journal will publish an article-length version. While these fears are sometimes justified, the evidence suggests that in most cases they are not.[4]

Universities expecting OA for ETDs teach the next generation of scholars how easy OA is to provide, how beneficial it is, and how routine it can be. They help cultivate lifelong habits of self-archiving. And they elicit better work. By giving authors a foreseeable, real audience beyond the dissertation committee, an OA policy strengthens existing incentives to do rigorous, original work.

If a university requires theses and dissertations to be new and significant works of scholarship, then it ought to expect them to be made public, just as it expects new and significant scholarship by faculty to be made public.

Sharing theses and dissertations that meet the school's high standard reflects well on the institution and benefits other researchers in the field. The university mission to advance research by young scholars has two steps, not one. First, help students produce good work, and then help others find, use, and build on that good work.

5.3   Books[5]

The OA movement focuses on journal articles because journals don't pay authors for their articles. This frees article authors to consent to OA without losing money. By contrast, book authors either earn royalties or hope to earn royalties.

Because the line between royalty-free and royalty-producing literature is bright (and life is short), many OA activists focus exclusively on journal articles and leave books aside. I recommend a different tactic: treat journal articles as low-hanging fruit, but treat books as higher-hanging fruit rather than forbidden fruit. There are even reasons to think that OA for some kinds of books is easier to attain than OA for journal articles.

The scope of OA should be determined by author consent, not genre. Imagine an author of a journal article who withholds consent to OA. The economic door is open but the author is not walking through it. This helps us see that relinquishing revenue is only relevant when it leads to consent, and consent suffices whether or not it's based on relinquishing revenue. It follows that if authors of royalty-producing genres, like books, consent to OA, then we'll have the same basis for OA to books that we have for OA to articles.

Even if books are higher-hanging fruit, they're not out of reach. Two arguments are increasingly successful in persuading book authors to consent to OA.

1. Royalties on most scholarly monographs range between zero and meager. If your royalties are better than that, congratulations. (I've earned book royalties; I'm grateful for them, and I wish all royalty-earning authors success.) The case for OA doesn't ask authors to make a new sacrifice or leave money on the table. It merely asks them to weigh the risk to their royalties against the benefit of OA, primarily the benefit of a larger audience and greater impact. For many book authors, the benefit will outweigh the risk. The benefit is large and the realistic prospect of royalties is low.

2. There is growing evidence that for some kinds of books, full-text OA editions boost the net sales of the priced, printed editions. OA may increase royalties rather than decrease them.

The first argument says that even if OA puts royalties at risk, the benefits might outweigh the risks. The second argument says that OA might not reduce royalties at all, and that conventional publication without an OA edition might be the greater risk. Both say, in effect, that authors should be empirical and realistic about this. Don't presume that your royalties will be high when there's evidence they will be low, and don't presume that OA will kill sales when there's evidence it could boost them.

Both arguments apply to authors, but the second applies to publishers as well. When authors have already transferred rights—and the OA decision—to a publisher, then the case rests on the second argument. A growing number of academic book publishers are either persuaded or so intrigued that they're experimenting.[6]

Many book authors want a print edition, badly. But the second argument is not only compatible with print but depends on print. The model is to give away the OA edition and sell a print edition, usually via print-on-demand (POD).[7]

Why would anyone buy a print book when the full text is OA? The answer is that many people don't want to read a whole book on a screen or gadget, and don't want to print out a whole book on their printer. They use OA editions for searching and sampling. When they discover a book that piques their curiosity or meets their personal standards of relevance and quality, they'll buy a copy. Or, many of them will buy a copy.

Evidence has been growing for about a decade that this phenomenon works for some books, or some kinds of books, even if it doesn't work for others. For example, it seems to work for books like novels and monographs, which readers want to read from beginning to end, or which they want to have on their shelves. It doesn't seem to work for books like encyclopedias, from which readers usually want just an occasional snippet.

One problem is running a controlled experiment, since we can't publish the same book with and without an OA edition to compare the sales. (If we publish a book initially without an OA edition and later add an OA edition, the time lag itself could affect sales.) Another variable is that ebook readers are becoming more and more consumer friendly. If the "net boost to sales" phenomenon is real, and if it depends on the ergonomic discomforts of reading digital books, then better gadgets may make the phenomenon disappear. If the net-boost phenomenon didn't depend on ergonomic hurdles to digital reading, or didn't depend entirely on them, then it might survive any sort of technological advances. There's a lot of experimenting still to do, and fortunately or unfortunately it must be done in a fast-changing environment.[8]

The U.S. National Academies Press began publishing full-text OA editions of its monographs alongside priced, printed editions in March 1994, which is ancient history in internet time. Over the years Michael Jensen, its director of web communications and director of publishing technologies, has published a series of articles showing that the OA editions increased the sales of the toll-access editions.[9]

In February 2007, the American Association of University Presses issued a Statement on Open Access in which it called for experiments with OA monographs and mixed OA/toll-access business models. By May 2011, the AAUP reported that 17 member presses, or 24 percent of its survey respondents, were already publishing full-text OA books.[10]

The question isn't whether some people will read the OA edition without buying the toll-access edition. Some will. The question isn't even whether more readers of the OA edition will buy the toll-access edition than not buy it. The question is whether more readers of the OA edition will buy the toll-access edition *than would have bought* the toll-access edition without the OA edition to alert them to its existence and help them evaluate its relevance and quality. If there are enough OA-inspired buyers, then it doesn't matter that there are also plenty of OA-satisfied nonbuyers.

Book authors and publishers who are still nervous could consent to delayed OA and release the OA edition only after six months or a year. During the time when the monograph is toll-access only, they could still provide OA excerpts and metadata to help readers and potential buyers find the book and start to assess it.

Even the youngest scholars today grew up in a world in which there were more print books in the average university library than gratis OA books online. But that ratio reversed around 2006, give or take. Today there are many more gratis OA books online than print books in the average academic library, and we're steaming toward the next crossover point when there will be many more gratis OA books online than print books in the world's largest libraries, academic or not.

A few years ago, those of us who focus on OA to journal literature were sure that journal articles were lower-hanging fruit than any kind of print books, including public-domain books. But we were wrong. There are still good reasons to make journal literature the strategic focus of the OA movement, and we're still making good progress on that front. But the lesson of the fast-moving book-scanning projects is that misunderstanding, inertia, and permission are more serious problems than digitization. The permission problem is solved for public-domain books. Digitizing them by the millions is a titanic technical undertaking, but it turns out to be a smaller problem than getting millions of copyrighted articles into OA journals or OA repositories, even when they're written by authors who can consent to OA without losing revenue. OA for new journal articles faces publisher resistance, print-era incentives, and misunderstandings in every category of stakeholders, including authors and publishers. As the late Jim Gray used to say, "May all your problems be technical."

5.4   Access to What?[11]

Not all the literature that researchers want to find, retrieve, and read should be called knowledge. We want access to serious proposals for knowledge even if they turn out to be false or incomplete. We want access to serious hypotheses even if we're still testing them and debating their merits. We want access to the data and analysis offered in support of the claims we're evaluating. We want access to all the arguments, evidence, and discussion. We want access to everything that could help us decide what to call knowledge, not just to the results that we agree to call knowledge. If access depended on the outcome of debate and inquiry, then access could not contribute to debate and inquiry.

We don't have a good name for this category larger than knowledge, but here I'll just call it research. Among other things, research includes knowledge and knowledge claims or proposals, hypotheses and conjectures, arguments and analysis, evidence and data, algorithms and methods, evaluation and interpretation, debate and discussion, criticism and dissent, summary and review. OA to research should be OA to the whole shebang. Inquiry and research suffer when we have access to anything less.

We want access to all the arguments, evidence, and discussion. We want access to everything that could help us decide what to call knowledge, not just to the results that we agree to call knowledge. If access depended on the outcome of debate and inquiry, then access could not contribute to debate and inquiry.

Some people call the journal literature the "minutes" of science, as if it were just a summary. But it's more than that. If the minutes of a meeting summarize a discussion, the journal literature is a large part of the discussion itself. Moreover, in an age of conferences, preprint servers, blogs, wikis, databases, listservs, and email, the journal literature is not the whole discussion. Wikipedia aspires to provide OA to a summary of knowledge, and (wisely) refuses to accept original research. But the larger OA movement wants OA to knowledge and original research themselves, as well as the full discussion about what we know and what we don't. It wants OA to the primary and secondary sources where knowledge is taking shape through a messy process that is neither consistent (as it works through the clash of conflicting hypotheses) nor stable (as it discards weak claims and considers new ones that appear stronger). The messiness and instability are properties of a discussion, not properties of the minutes of a discussion. The journal literature isn't just a report on the process but a major channel of the process itself. And not incidentally, OA is valuable not just for making the process public but for facilitating the process and making it more effective, expeditious, transparent, and global.[12]

To benefit from someone's research, we need access to it, and for this purpose it doesn't matter whether the research is in the sciences or humanities. We need access to medical or physical research before we can use it to tackle a cure for malaria or devise a more efficient solar panel. We need access to an earthquake prediction before we can use it to plan emergency responses.[13] And we need access to literary and philosophical research in order to understand a difficult passage in Homer or the strength of a response to epistemological skepticism.

For this kind of utility, the relevant comparison is not between pure and applied research or between the sciences and humanities. The relevant comparison is between any kind of research when OA and the same kind of research when locked behind price and permission barriers. Whether a given line of research serves wellness or wisdom, energy or enlightenment, protein synthesis or public safety, OA helps it serve those purposes faster, better, and more universally.

5.5   Access for Whom?

Answer: human beings and machines.

5.5.1   OA for Lay Readers[14]

Some have opposed OA on the ground that not everyone needs it, which is a little like opposing the development of a safe and effective new medicine on the ground that not every one needs it. It's easy to agree that not everyone needs it. But in the case of OA, there's no easy way to identify those who do and those who don't. In addition, there's no easy way, and no reason, to deliver it only to those who need it and deny it to everyone else.

OA allows us to provide access to everyone who cares to have access, without patronizing guesswork about who really wants it, who really deserves it, and who would really benefit from it. Access for everyone with an internet connection helps authors, by enlarging their audience and impact, and helps readers who want access and who might have been excluded by central planners trying to decide in advance whom to enfranchise. The idea is to stop thinking of knowledge as a commodity to meter out to deserving customers, and to start thinking of it as a public good, especially when it is given away by its authors, funded with public money, or both.[15]

Some lobbyists for toll-access publishers argue, in good faith or bad, that the goal of OA is to bring access to lay readers. This sets up their counter-argument that lay readers don't care to read cutting-edge research and wouldn't understand it if they tried. Some publishers go a step further and argue that access to research would harm lay readers.[16]

This is a two-step argument, that OA is primarily for lay readers and that lay readers don't need it. Each step is false. The first step overlooks the unmet demand for access by professional researchers, as if all professionals who wanted access already had it, and the second overlooks the unmet demand for access by lay readers, as if lay readers had no use for access.

One reason to think the first step is put forward in bad faith is that it overlooks the very conspicuous fact that the OA movement is driven by researchers who are emphatic about wanting the benefits of OA for themselves. It also overlooks the evidence of wide and widespread access gaps even for professional researchers. (See section 2.1 on problems.)

The problem with the second step is presumption. How does anyone know in advance the level of demand for peer-reviewed research among lay readers? When peer-reviewed literature is toll-access and expensive, then lack of access by lay readers and consumers doesn't show lack of demand, any more than lack of access to Fort Knox shows lack of demand for gold. We have to remove access barriers before we can distinguish lack of access from lack of interest. The experiment has been done, more than once. When the U.S. National Library of Medicine converted to OA in 2004, for example, visitors to its web site increased more than a hundredfold.[17]

A common related argument is that lay readers surfing the internet are easily misled by unsupported claims, refuted theories, anecdotal evidence, and quack remedies. Even if true, however, it's an argument for rather than against expanding online access to peer-reviewed research.

If we're really worried about online dreck, we should dilute it with high-quality research rather than leave the dreck unchallenged and uncorrected.

Many of us medical nonprofessionals—who may be professionals in another field—want access to medical research in order to read about our own conditions or the conditions of family members. But even if few fall into that category, most of us still want access for our doctors, nurses, and hospitals. We still want access for the nonprofit advocacy organizations working on our behalf, such as the AIDS Vaccine Advocacy Coalition, the Cystinosis Research Network, or the Spina Bifida Association of America. And in turn, doctors, nurses, hospitals, and advocacy organizations want access for laboratory researchers. As I argued earlier (section 1.2), OA benefits researchers directly and benefits everyone else indirectly by benefiting researchers.[18]

A May 2006 Harris poll showed that an overwhelming majority of Americans wanted OA for publicly funded research. 83 percent wanted it for their doctors and 82 percent wanted it for everyone. 81 percent said it would help medical patients and their families cope with chronic illness and disability. 62 percent said it would speed up the discovery of new cures. For each poll question, a fairly large percentage of respondents checked "neither agree nor disagree" (between 13 and 30 percent), which meant that only tiny minorities disagreed with the OA propositions. Only 3 percent didn't want OA for their doctors, 4 percent didn't want it for themselves, and 5 percent didn't think it would help patients or their families.[19]

The ratio of professional to lay readers of peer-reviewed research undoubtedly varies from field to field. But for the purpose of OA policy, it doesn't matter what the ratio is in any field. What matters is that neither group has sufficient access today, when most research journals are toll-access. Professional researchers don't have sufficient access through their institutional libraries because subscription prices are rising faster than library budgets, even at the wealthiest libraries in the world. Motivated lay readers don't have sufficient access because few public libraries subscribe to any peer-reviewed research journals, and none to the full range.[20]

The argument against access for lay readers suffers from more than false assumptions about unmet demand. Either it concedes or doesn't concede that OA is desirable for professional researchers. If it doesn't, then it should argue first against the strongest opponent and try to make the case against OA for professionals. But if it does concede that OA for professionals is a good idea, then it wants to build a selection system for deciding who deserves access, and an authentication system for sorting the sheep from the goats. Part of the beauty of OA is that providing access to everyone is cheaper and easier than providing access to some and blocking access to others. We should only raise costs and pay for the apparatus of exclusion when there's a very good reason to do so.[21]

5.5.2 OA for Machines[22]

We also want access for machines. I don't mean the futuristic altruism in which kindly humans want to help curious machines answer their own questions. I mean something more selfish. We're well into the era in which serious research is mediated by sophisticated software. If our machines don't have access, then we don't have access. Moreover, if we can't get access for our machines, then we lose a momentous opportunity to enhance access with processing.

Think about the size of the body of literature to which you have access, online and off. Now think realistically about the subset to which you'd have practical access if you couldn't use search engines, or if search engines couldn't index the literature you needed.

Information overload didn't start with the internet. The internet does vastly increase the volume of work to which we have access, but at the same time it vastly increases our ability to find what we need. We zero in on the pieces that deserve our limited time with the aid of powerful software, or more precisely, powerful software with access. Software helps us learn what exists, what's new, what's relevant, what others find relevant, and what others are saying about it. Without these tools, we couldn't cope with information overload. Or we'd have to redefine "coping" as artificially reducing the range of work we are allowed to consider, investigate, read, or retrieve.[23]

Some publishers have seriously argued that high toll-access journal prices and limited library budgets help us cope with information overload, as if the literature we can't afford always coincides with the literature we don't need. But of course much that is relevant to our projects is unaffordable to our libraries. If any problems are intrinsic to a very large and fast-growing, accessible corpus of literature, they don't arise from size itself, or size alone, but from limitations on our discovery tools. With OA and sufficiently powerful tools, we could always find and retrieve what we needed. Without sufficiently powerful tools, we could not. Replacing OA with high-priced toll access would only add new obstacles to research, even if it simultaneously made the accessible corpus small enough for weaker discovery tools to master. In Clay Shirky's concise formulation, the real problem is not information overload but filter failure.[24]

OA is itself a spectacular inducement for software developers to create useful tools to filter what we can find. As soon as the tools are finished, they apply to a free, useful, and fast-growing body of online literature. Conversely, useful tools optimized for OA literature create powerful incentives for authors and publishers to open up their work. As soon as their work is OA, a vast array of powerful tools make it more visible and useful. In the early days of OA, shortages on each side created a vicious circle: the small quantity of OA literature provided little incentive to develop new tools optimized for making it more visible and useful, and the dearth of powerful tools provided little extra incentive to make new work OA. But today a critical mass of OA literature invites the development of useful tools, and a critical mass of useful tools gives authors and publishers another set of reasons to make their work OA.

All digital literature, OA or toll access, is machine-readable and supports new and useful kinds of processing. But toll-access literature minimizes that opportunity by shrinking the set of inputs with access fees, password barriers, copyright restrictions, and software locks. By removing price and permission barriers, OA maximizes this opportunity and spawns an ecosystem of tools for searching, indexing, mining, summarizing, translating, querying, linking, recommending, alerting, mashing-up, and other kinds of processing, not to mention myriad forms of crunching and connecting that we can't even imagine today. One bedrock purpose of OA is to give these research-enhancing, utility-amplifying tools the widest possible scope of operation.

In this sense, the ultimate promise of OA is not to provide free online texts for human reading, even if that is the highest-value end use. The ultimate promise of OA is to provide free online data for software acting as the antennae, prosthetic eyeballs, research assistants, and personal librarians of all serious researchers.

Opening research literature for human users also opens it for software to crunch the literature for the benefit of human users. We can even hope that OA itself will soon be old hat, taken for granted by a new generation of tools and services that depend on it. As those tools and services come along, they will be the hot story and they will deserve to be. Technologists will note that they all depend on OA, and historians will note that OA itself was not easily won.[25]

COPYRIGHT

OA could be implemented badly so that it infringes copyright.[1] But so could conventional publishing. Both OA and toll access have long since discovered the same recipe for avoiding copyright problems: For sufficiently old works, rely on the public domain, and for newer works under copyright, rely on copyright-holder consent. This shouldn't be surprising. Toll-access publishers don't have a shortcut to copyright compliance just because they charge money for access, and OA publishers don't face an extra hurdle to copyright compliance just because they don't charge for access. Copyright protects the revenue streams of those who choose to charge for access but doesn't compel anyone to charge for access.

When researchers publish in OA journals, the permission problem is easily solved. Either the author retains the key rights and the publisher obtains the author's permission, or the author transfers the key rights to the publisher and the publisher uses them to authorize OA.

Toll-access journals don't make their articles OA, of course, but more often than not they give blanket permission for authors to make their peer-reviewed manuscripts green OA. (See section 3.1 on green OA.)

When authors transfer all rights to the publisher, then they also transfer the OA decision to the publisher. When the publisher doesn't already allow green OA, then authors must ask permission to make their work OA. However, many publishers who don't give blanket permission for green OA will agree to case-by-case requests. (For example, before Elsevier started giving blanket permission in 2004, its policy was to agree to essentially all case-by-case requests.)

When authors submit work to toll-access journals but retain the right to authorize OA, then the OA decision belongs to them. Publishers may refuse to publish their work, of course, but they seldom do so merely because of rights retention when authors are following a policy of their funder or employer. As noted (in chapter 4 on policies), the NIH has one of the strongest rights-retention OA policies anywhere, and to date not a single surveyed publisher refuses to publish NIH-funded authors on account of its mandatory OA policy.[2]

Publishers who refuse to publish rights-retaining authors are not asserting copyright. They are asserting an independent, background right to refuse to publish any work for any reason. (I support this right and would never

Authors who retain rights don't violate rights belonging to publishers; they merely prevent publishers from acquiring those rights in the first place.

want to see publishers lose it.) Authors who retain rights don't violate rights belonging to publishers; they merely prevent publishers from acquiring those rights in the first place. When rights-retaining authors make their work OA, publishers can't complain that OA infringes a right they possess, only that it would infringe a right they wished they possessed. Publishers who face rights retention face hard bargaining, not infringement. Publishers still have a remedy, but it's the remedy to hard bargaining (just say no), not the remedy to infringement (sue or threaten to sue).

We can see this from another angle. If the NIH policy violated copyright law, publishers would have sued. But instead, their strongest response has been to support a bill amending U.S. copyright law to make NIH-style policies unlawful. That's a concession that the NIH policy is lawful under current law. In that sense, strong rights-retention policies are not only lawful but battle-tested.[3]

Of course authors may retain rights on their own, even when not required to do so by a funder or university policy. But when authors stand alone, they have very little bargaining power against publishers who demand the rights as a condition of publication. One of the practical benefits of strong rights-retention policies is that they amplify the author's bargaining power and tend to elicit publisher accommodation.

When authors retain the right to authorize OA, and use that right to authorize OA, then the resulting OA is authorized by the copyright holder. The fact that the decision is from the author rather than the publisher makes it unconventional, but not unlawful, insufficient, or legally dubious.

Authors who retain the right to authorize OA may still transfer all other rights to publishers, and typically do. In these cases, publishers may not acquire all the rights they want, or all the rights they formerly acquired. But they acquire all the rights they need for publishing, and they have undiminished power to enforce the rights they acquire.

This solution works because funders and universities are upstream from publishers. In the case of funders, grantees sign their funding contracts before they sign their publishing contracts. In the case of universities, faculty members vote to authorize university-hosted OA to their future publications before they sign their future publishing contracts.

OA journals obtain the needed permission through a publishing contract with the author, just as conventional journals do. But because OA journals aren't trying to protect sales revenue, they needn't prohibit copying and redistribution. On the contrary, OA journals share the author's interest in maximizing impact by maximizing distribution and reuse rights. Hence, OA journals may request fewer rights from authors and allow more uses than toll-access journals do.[4]

Conventional wisdom holds that authors need copyright to give them an incentive to write. Others can debate whether this is true for nonacademic authors like novelists and journalists. (L. Ray Patterson liked to point out that it wasn't true for Chaucer, Shakespeare, or Milton.[5]) But there are two reasons why it's simply false for authors of research articles. First, authors of research articles are not paid. When money is even part of an author's incentive, copyright fortifies the incentive by giving authors a temporary monopoly on their work and the revenue stream arising from it. Without copyright, unauthorized copies might kill the market for authorized copies and reduce sales. But all this is irrelevant to authors who write for impact, not for money, and who voluntarily forgo royalties.

Second, authors of research articles traditionally transferred copyright to publishers. Hence, copyrights on research articles traditionally protected publishers, not authors. If the conventional wisdom about incentives were true for research articles, then transferring the rights to publishers would have diminished author productivity. But that did not happen. On the contrary, scholars have always had independent incentives to write journal articles, such as knowledge sharing, reputation building, and creating a portfolio for promotion and tenure. They never expected revenue from their articles, never needed a temporary monopoly on that revenue, rarely even knew what the revenue was, and never wrote for the purpose of generating revenue for the publishers who actually owned the copyrights in their work.

Conventional wisdom holds that authors need copyright to give them an incentive to write. Others can debate whether this is true for nonacademic authors like novelists and journalists. (L. Ray Patterson liked to point out that it wasn't true for Chaucer, Shakespeare, or Milton.)

Because scholars don't earn royalties on their research articles, they would not be hurt by dramatic copyright reforms designed to restore balance between copyright holders and users—not that such reforms are likely any time soon. Publishers who pretend to speak for authors in defending the current imbalance in copyright law speak for authors of royalty-producing literature. Authors of royalty-free literature have very different interests.

ECONOMICS

Many publishers who oppose OA concede that OA is better for research and researchers than toll access.[1] They merely object that we can't pay for it. But we can pay for it.

The first major study of the economic impact of OA policies was conducted by John Houghton and Peter Sheehan in 2006. Using conservative estimates that a nation's gross expenditure on research and development (GERD) brings social returns of 50 percent, and that OA increases access and efficiency by 5 percent, Houghton and Sheehan calculated that a transition to OA would not only pay for itself, but add $1.7 billion/year to the UK economy and $16 billion/year to the U.S. economy. A later study focusing on Australia used the more conservative estimate that GERD brings social returns of only 25 percent, but still found that the bottom-line economic benefits of OA for publicly funded research were 51 times greater than the costs.[2]

Independent confirmation of Houghton's results came in a major study released in April 2011, commissioned by the UK Joint Information Systems Committee, Publishing Research Consortium, Research Information Network, Research Libraries UK, and the Wellcome Trust. After studying five scenarios for improving research access, it concluded that green and gold OA "offer the greatest potential to policy-makers in promoting access. Both have positive, and potentially high, BCRs [benefit-cost ratios]. . . ."[3]

The same study noted that "the infrastructure for Green [OA] has largely already been built" and therefore that "increasing access by this route is especially cost-effective. . . ." I can add that repositories scale up more easily than journals to capture unmet demand, and that depositing in a repository costs the depositor nothing. For all these reasons, I'll focus in this chapter on how to pay for gold OA (journals), not how to pay for green OA (repositories).

Before turning to gold OA, however, I should note that there are widely varying estimates in the literature on what it costs a university to run an institutional repository. The divergence reflects the fact that repositories can serve many different purposes, and that some repositories serve more of them than others. If the minimum purpose is to host OA copies of faculty articles, and if faculty deposit their own articles, then the cost is minimal. But a repository is a general-purpose tool, and once launched there are

OA journals pay their bills the way broadcast television and radio stations do—not through advertising or pledge drives, but through a simple generalization on advertising and pledge drives. Those with an interest in disseminating the content pay the production costs upfront so that access can be free of charge for everyone with the right equipment.

good reasons for it to take on other responsibilities, such as long-term preservation, assisting faculty with digitization, permissions, and deposits, and hosting many other sorts of content, such as theses and dissertations, books or book chapters, conference proceedings, courseware, campus publications, digitized special collections, and administrative records. If the average repository is a significant expense today, the reason is that the average repository is doing significantly more than the minimum.[4]

OA journals pay their bills the way broadcast television and radio stations do—not through advertising or pledge drives, but through a simple generalization on advertising and pledge drives. Those with an interest in disseminating the content pay the production costs upfront so that access can be free of charge for everyone with the right equipment. Elsewhere I've called this the "some pay for all" model.[5]

Some OA journals have a subsidy from a university, library, foundation, society, museum, or government agency. Other OA journals charge a publication fee on accepted articles, to be paid by the author or the author's sponsor (employer or funder). The party paying the subsidy or fee covers the journal's expenses and readers pay nothing.

OA journals that charge publication fees tend to waive them in cases of economic hardship, and journals with institutional subsidies tend not to charge publication fees.

OA journals can diversify their funding and get by on lower subsidies, or lower fees, if they also have revenue from print editions, advertising, priced add-ons, or auxiliary services. Some institutions and consortia arrange fee discounts, or purchase annual memberships that include fee waivers or discounts for all affiliated researchers.

Models that work well in some fields and nations may not work as well in others. No one claims that one size fits all. There's still room for creativity in finding ways to pay the costs of a peer-reviewed OA journal, and many smart and motivated people are exploring different possibilities. Journals announce new variations almost every week, and we're far from exhausting our cleverness and imagination.[6]

Green OA may suffer from invisibility, but gold OA does not. On the contrary, researchers who don't know about OA repositories still understand that there are OA journals. Sometimes the visibility gap is so large that researchers, journalists, and policy-makers conclude that all OA is gold OA (see section 3.1 on green and gold OA). As a result, most researchers who think about the benefits of OA think about the benefits of gold OA. Here, at least, the news is good. The most comprehensive survey to date shows that an overwhelming 89 percent of researchers from all fields believe that OA journals are beneficial to their fields.[7]

Apart from the myth that all OA is gold OA, the most common myth about gold OA is that all OA journals charge "author fees" or use an "author-pays" business model. There are three mistakes here. The first is to assume that there is only one business model for OA journals, when there are many. The second is to assume that charging an upfront fee means authors are the ones expected to pay it. The third is to assume that all or even most OA journals charge upfront fees. In fact, most OA journals (70 percent) charge no upfront or author-side fees at all. By

Terminology

The terms "author fees" and "author pays" are specious and damaging. They're false for the majority of OA journals, which charge no fees. They're also misleading even for fee-based OA journals, where nearly nine times out of ten the fees are not paid by authors themselves. It's more accurate to speak of "publication fees," "processing fees," or "author-side fees." The first two don't specify the payor, and the third merely specifies that the payment comes from the author side of the transaction, rather than the reader side, without implying that it must come from authors themselves.

contrast, most toll-access journals (75 percent) do charge author-side fees. Moreover, even within the minority of fee-based OA journals, only 12 percent of those authors end up paying the fees out of pocket. Almost 90 percent of the time, the fees at fee-based journals are waived or paid by sponsors on behalf of authors.[8]

The false beliefs that most OA journals charge author-side fees and that most toll-access journals don't have caused several kinds of harm. They scare authors away from OA journals. They support the misconception that gold OA excludes indigent authors. When we add in the background myth that all OA is gold OA, this misconception suggests that OA as such—and not just gold OA—excludes indigent authors.

These false beliefs also support the insinuation that OA journals are more likely than non-OA journals to compromise on peer review. But if charging author-side fees for accepted papers really creates an incentive to lower standards, in order to rake in more fees, then most toll-access journals are guilty and most OA journals are not. In fact, however, when OA journals do charge author-side fees, they create firewalls between their financial and editorial operations. For example, most fee-based OA journals will waive their fees in cases of economic hardship, and take pains to prevent editors and referees engaged in peer review from knowing whether or not an author has requested a fee waiver. By contrast, at toll-access journals levying author-side page or color charges, editors generally know that accepted papers will entail revenue.[9]

The false belief that most OA journals charge author-side fees also infects studies in which authors misinform survey subjects before surveying them. In effect: "At OA journals, authors pay to be published; now let me ask you a series of questions about your attitude toward OA journals."

Finally, this false belief undermines calculations about who would bear the financial brunt if we made a general transition from toll-access journals to OA journals. A handful of studies have calculated that after a general conversion of peer-reviewed journals to OA, high-output universities would pay more in author-side fees than they pay now in subscriptions. These calculations make at least two assumptions unjustified by present facts or trends: that all OA journals would charge fees, and that all fees would be paid by universities.[10]

There are two kinds of OA journals, full and hybrid. Full OA journals provide OA to all their research articles. Hybrid OA journals provide OA to some and toll-access to others, when the choice is the author's rather than the editor's. Most hybrid OA journals charge a publication fee for the OA option. Authors who can find the money get immediate OA, and those who can't or prefer not to, get toll access. (Many hybrid OA journals provide OA to all their articles after some time period, such as a year.) Some hybrid OA journals promise to reduce subscription prices in proportion to author uptake of the OA option, that is, to charge subscribers only for the toll-access articles. But most hybrid journal publishers don't make this promise and "double dip" by charging subscription fees and publication fees for the same OA articles.[11]

Hybrid OA is very low-risk for publishers. If the OA option has low uptake, the publisher loses nothing and still has subscription revenue. If it has high uptake, the publisher has subscription revenue for the conventional articles, publication fees for the OA articles, and sometimes both at once for the OA articles. Hence, the model has spread far and fast. The Professional/Scholarly Publishing division of the Association of American Publishers reported in 2011 that 74 percent of surveyed journals offering some form of OA in 2009 offered hybrid OA. At the same time, SHERPA listed more than 90 publishers offering hybrid OA options, including all of the largest publishers. Despite its spread, hybrid OA journals do little or nothing to help researchers, libraries, or publishers. The average rate of uptake for the OA option at hybrid journals is just 2 percent.[12]

The chief virtue of hybrid OA journals is that they give publishers some firsthand experience with the economics and logistics of OA publishing. But the economics are artificial, since hybrid OA publishers have no incentive to increase author uptake and make the model succeed. The publishers always have subscriptions to fall back on. More-over, an overwhelming majority of full-OA journals charge no publication fees and the overwhelming majority of hybrid-OA journals never gain firsthand experience with no-fee business models.[13]

A growing number of for-profit OA publishers are making profits, and a growing number of nonprofit OA publishers are breaking even or making surpluses. Two different business models drive these sustainable publishing programs. BioMed Central makes profits and the Public Library of Science makes surpluses by charging publication fees. MedKnow makes profits without charging publication fees by selling priced print editions of its OA journals.[14]

Fee-based OA journals tend to work best in fields where most research is funded, and no-fee journals tend to work best in fields and countries where comparatively little research is funded. The successes of these two business models give hope that gold OA can be sustainable in every discipline.

Every kind of peer-reviewed journal can become more sustainable by reducing costs. Although peer review is generally performed by unpaid volunteers, organizing or facilitating peer review is an expense. The journal must select referees, distribute files to referees, monitor who has what, track progress, nag dawdlers, collect comments and share them with the right people, facilitate communication, distinguish versions, and collect data on acceptances and rejections. One powerful way to reduce costs without reducing quality is to use free and open-source journal management software to automate the clerical tasks on this list.

The leader in this field is Open Journal Systems from the Public Knowledge Project, but there are more than a dozen other open-source packages. While OJS or other open-source software could benefit even toll-access journals, their use is concentrated among OA journals. OJS alone has more than 9,000 installations (though not all are used for managing journals). This is not merely an example of how one openness movement can help another but also of how fearing openness can lead conventional publishers to forgo financial benefits and leave money on the table.[15]

There are reasons to think that OA journals cost less to produce than toll-access journals of the same quality. OA journals dispense with subscription management (soliciting, negotiating, tracking, renewing subscribers), dispense with digital rights management (authenticating users, distinguishing authorized from unauthorized, blocking access to unauthorized), eliminate legal fees for licensing (drafting, negotiating, monitoring, and enforcing restrictive licenses), and reduce or eliminate marketing. In their place they add back little more than the cost of collecting publication fees or institutional subsidies. Several studies and OA publishers have testified to these lower costs.[16]

We shouldn't count the savings from dropping print, since most toll-access journals in the sciences have already dropped their print editions and those in the humanities are moving in the same direction.

We should be suspicious when large, venerable, conventional publishers say that in their experience the economics of OA publishing don't work. Print-era publishers retooling for digital, and toll-access publishers retooling for OA, will inevitably realize smaller savings from OA than lean, mean OA start-ups without legacy equipment, personnel, or overhead from the age of print and subscriptions.

About one-quarter of all peer-reviewed journals today are OA. Like toll-access journals, some are in the black and thriving and some are in the red and struggling. However, the full range of OA journals begins to look like a success story when we consider that the vast majority of the money needed to support peer-reviewed journals is currently tied up in subscriptions to conventional journals. OA journals have reached their current numbers and quality despite the extraordinary squeeze on budgets devoted to the support of peer-reviewed journals.

Even if OA journals had the same production costs as toll-access journals, there's enough money in the system to pay for peer-reviewed OA journals in every niche where we currently have peer-reviewed toll-access journals, and at the same level of quality. In fact, there's more than enough, since we wouldn't have to pay publisher profit margins surpassing those at ExxonMobil. Jan Velterop, the former publisher of BioMed Central, once said that OA publishing can be profitable but will "bring profit margins more in line with the added value."[17]

To support a full range of high-quality OA journals, we don't need new money. We only need to redirect money we're currently spending on peer-reviewed toll-access journals.[18] There are many kinds of redirection. One is the voluntary conversion of toll-access journals to OA. Conversion could be a journal's grudging response to declining library budgets for toll-access journals and exclusion from the big deals that take the lion's share of library budgets. It could be a grudging response to its own past price increases and rising levels of green OA (see chapter 8 on casualties). Or it could be a hopeful and enthusiastic desire to achieve the benefits of OA for authors (greater audience and impact), readers (freedom from price and permission barriers), and publishers themselves (increased readership, citations, submissions, and quality).

Another kind of redirection is the rise of OA journal funds at universities. Even during times of declining budgets, libraries are setting aside money to pay publication fees at fee-based OA journals. The funds help faculty choose OA journals for their new work and help build a sustainable alternative to toll-access journals.[19]

Redirection is also taking place on a large scale, primarily through CERN's SCOAP3 project (Sponsoring Consortium for Open Access Publishing in Particle Physics). SCOAP3 is an ambitious plan to convert all the major toll-access journals in particle physics to OA, redirect the money formerly spent on reader-side subscription fees to author-side publication fees, and reduce the overall price to the journal-supporting institutions. It's a peaceful revolution based on negotiation, consent, and self-interest. After four years of patiently building up budget pledges from libraries around the world, SCOAP3 entered its implementation phase in in April 2011.[20]

If SCOAP3 succeeds, it won't merely prove that CERN can pull off ambitious projects, which we already knew. It will prove that this particular ambitious project has an underlying win-win logic convincing to stakeholders. Some of the factors explaining the success of SCOAP3 to date are physics-specific, such as the small number of targeted journals, the green OA culture in physics embraced even by toll-access publishers, and the dominance of CERN. Other factors are not physics-specific, such as the evident benefits for research institutions, libraries, funders, and publishers. A success in particle physics would give hope that the model could be lifted and adapted to other fields without their own CERN-like institutions to pave the way. Other fields would not need CERN-like money or dominance so much as CERN-like convening power to bring the stakeholders to the table. Then the win-win logic would have a chance to take over from there.

Mark Rowse, former CEO of Ingenta, sketched another strategy for large-scale redirection in December 2003. A publisher could "flip" its toll-access journals to OA at one stroke by reinterpreting the payments it receives from university libraries as publication fees for a group of authors rather than subscription fees for a group of readers. One advantage over SCOAP3 is that the Rowsean flip can be tried one journal or one publisher at a time, and doesn't require discipline-wide coordination. It could also scale up to the largest publishers or the largest coalitions of publishers.[21]

We have to be imaginative but we don't have to improvise. There are some principles we can try to follow. Money freed up by the cancellation or conversion of peer-reviewed TA journals should be spent first on peer-reviewed OA journals, to ensure the continuation of peer review. Large-scale redirection is more efficient than small-scale redirection. Peaceful revolution through negotiation and self-interest is more amicable and potentially more productive than adaptation forced by falling asteroids.

For the record, I advocate redirecting money freed up by cancellations or conversions, not canceling journals in order to free up money (except with SCOAP3 or Rowse-like consent and negotiation). This may look like hair-splitting, but the difference is neither small nor subtle. It's roughly the difference between having great expectations and planning to kill your parents.

CASUALTIES

Will a general shift to OA leave casualties?[1] For example, will rising levels of green OA trigger cancellations of toll-access journals?

This question matters for those publishers (not all publishers) who fear the answer is yes and for those activists (not all activists) who hope the answer is yes. So far, unfortunately, it doesn't have a simple yes-or-no answer, and most discussions replace evidence with fearful or hopeful predictions.

The primary drivers of green OA are policies at universities and funding agencies. Remember, all university policies allow publishers to protect themselves at will. (See section 4.1 on policies.) For example, universities with loophole or deposit mandates will not provide green OA when publishers do not allow it. Universities with Harvard-style rights-retention mandates will not provide OA when authors obtain waivers or when publishers require authors to obtain waivers as a condition of publication.

Hence, publishers who worry about the effect of university OA policies on subscriptions have the remedy in their own hands. Faculty needn't paternalize publishers by voting down OA policies when publishers can protect themselves whenever they see the need to do so. The experience at Harvard since February 2008 is that very few publishers see the need to do so. Fewer than a handful systematically require waivers from Harvard authors.

This chapter, then, focuses on the strongest green OA mandates at funding agencies, like the Wellcome Trust and NIH, which allow no opt-outs for publishers or grantees. Will strong green OA policies of that kind trigger cancellations of toll-access journals? Here are 10 parts of any complete answer.

1. Nobody knows yet how green OA policies will affect journal subscriptions.

Rising levels of green OA may trigger toll-access journal cancellations, or they may not. So far they haven't.

2. The evidence from physics is the most relevant.

Physics has the highest levels and longest history of green OA. The evidence from physics to date is that high levels of green OA don't cause journal cancellations. On the contrary, the relationship between arXiv (the OA repository for physics) and toll-access physics journals is more symbiotic than antagonistic.

Physicists have been self-archiving since 1991, far longer than in any other field. In some subfields, such as particle physics, the rate of OA archiving approaches 100 percent, far higher than in any other field. If high-volume green OA caused journal cancellations, we'd see the effect first in physics. But it hasn't happened. Two leading publishers of physics journals, the American Physical Society (APS) and Institute of Physics (IOP), have publicly acknowledged that they've seen no cancellations attributable to OA archiving. In fact, the APS and IOP have not only made peace with arXiv but now accept submissions from it and even host their own mirrors of it.[2]

3. Other fields may not behave like physics.

We won't know more until the levels of green OA in other fields approach those in physics.

It would definitely help to understand why the experience in physics has gone as it has and how far it might predict the experience in other fields. But so far it's fair to say that we don't know all the variables and that publishers who oppose green OA mandates are not among those showing a serious interest in them. When publisher lobbyists argue that high-volume green OA will undermine toll-access journal subscriptions, they don't offer evidence, don't acknowledge the countervailing evidence from physics, don't rebut the evidence from physics, and don't qualify their own conclusions in light of it. They would act more like scientific publishers if they acknowledged the evidence from physics and then argued, as well as they could, either that the experience in physics will change or that fields other than physics will have a different experience.

An October 2004 editorial in *The Lancet* (an Elsevier journal) called on the publishing lobby to do better. "[A]s editors of a journal that publishes research funded by the NIH, we disagree with [Association of American Publishers President Patricia Schroeder's] central claim. Widening access to research [through green OA mandates] is unlikely to bring the edifice of scientific publishing crashing down. Schroeder provides no evidence that it would do so; she merely asserts the threat. This style of rebuttal will not do. . . ."[3]

For more than eight years, green OA mandates have applied to research in many fields outside physics. These mandates are natural experiments and we're still monitoring their effects. At Congressional hearings in 2008 and 2010, legislators asked publishers directly whether green OA was triggering cancellations. In both cases, publishers pointed to decreased downloads but not to increased cancellations.[4]

Physicists have been self-archiving since 1991, far longer than in any other field. In some sub-fields, such as particle physics, the rate of OA archiving approaches 100 percent, far higher than in any other field. If high-volume green OA caused journal cancellations, we'd see the effect first in physics. But it hasn't happened.

4. There is evidence that green OA decreases downloads from publishers' web sites.

When users know about OA and toll-access editions of the same article, many will prefer to click through to the OA edition, either because they aren't affiliated with a subscribing institution or because authentication is a hassle. Moreover, when users find an OA edition, most stop looking. But decreased downloads are not the same thing as decreased or canceled subscriptions.

Moreover, decreased downloads of toll-access editions from publisher web sites are not the same thing as decreased downloads overall. No one suggests that green OA leads to decreased overall downloads, that is, fewer readers and less reading. On the contrary, the same evidence suggesting that OA increases citation impact also suggests that it increases readers and reading.[5]

5. Most publishers voluntarily permit green OA.

Supplementing the natural experiments of green OA mandates are the natural experiments of publishers who voluntarily permit green OA. The Nature Publishing Group is more conservative than most toll-access publishers by requiring a six-month embargo on green OA, but more progressive than most by positively encouraging green OA. NPG reported the latest results of its multidisciplinary natural experiment in January 2011: "We have, to date, found author self-archiving compatible with subscription business models, and so we have been actively encouraging self-archiving since 2005."[6]

This or something similar to it must be the experience of the majority of toll-access publishers who voluntarily permit green OA. Even if they don't actively encourage green OA, most permit it without embargo. If they found that it triggered cancellations, they would stop.

6. Green OA mandates leave standing at least four library incentives to maintain their subscriptions to toll-access journals.

Even the strongest no-loophole, no-waiver policies preserve incentives to maintain toll-access journal subscriptions.

First, all funder OA mandates include an embargo period to protect publishers. For example, the OA mandates at the Research Councils UK allow an embargo of up to six months after publication. The NIH allows an embargo of up to twelve months. Libraries wanting to provide immediate access will still have an incentive to subscribe.

Second, all funder OA mandates apply to the final version of the author's peer-reviewed manuscript, not to the published version. If the journal provides copyediting after peer review, then the policies do not apply to the copyedited version, let alone to the formatted, paginated published edition. Libraries wanting to provide access to copyedited published editions will still have an incentive to subscribe.

The purpose of these two policy provisions is precisely to protect publishers against cancellations. They are deliberate concessions to publishers, adopted voluntarily by funding agencies as compromises with the public interest in immediate OA to the best editions. When we put the two together, we see that funder-mandated OA copies of peer-reviewed manuscripts won't compete with toll-access copies of the published editions for six to twelve months, and there will never be OA copies of the more desirable published editions unless publishers voluntarily allow them. Publishers retain life-of-copyright exclusivity on the published editions. Even if OA archiving does eventually erode subscriptions outside physics, publishers have longer and better protection from these effects than their lobbyists ever acknowledge.

Third, funder OA mandates only apply to research articles, not to the many other kinds of content published in scholarly journals, such as letters, editorials, review articles, book reviews, announcements, news, conference information, and so on. Libraries wanting to provide access to these other kinds of content will still have an incentive to subscribe.

Fourth, funder OA mandates only apply to articles arising from research funded by the mandating agency. Very few journals publish nothing but articles from a single funder, or even from a set of funders all of whom have OA mandates. Libraries wanting to provide access to all the research articles in a journal, regardless of the sources of funding, will still have an incentive to subscribe. This incentive will weaken as more and more funders adopt OA mandates, but we're very far from universal funder mandates. As we get closer, unfunded research will still fall outside this category and the three other incentives above will still stand.

The Association of College and Research Libraries addressed subscription incentives in a 2004 open letter on the NIH policy: "We wish to emphasize, above all, that academic libraries will not cancel journal subscriptions as a result of this plan. . . . Even if libraries wished to consider the availability of NIH-funded articles when making journal cancellation decisions, they would have no reasonable way of determining what articles in specific journals would become openly accessible after the embargo period."[7]

7. Some studies bear on the question of whether increased OA archiving will increase journal cancellations.

In a 2006 study from the Publishing Research Consortium (PRC), Chris Beckett and Simon Inger asked 400 librarians about the relative weight of different factors in their decisions to cancel subscriptions. Other things being equal, the librarians preferred free content to priced content and short embargoes to longer ones. Publishers interpret this to mean that the rise of OA archiving will cause cancellations. The chief flaw with the study is its artificiality. For example, the survey did not ask about specific journals by name but only about resources with abstractly stipulated levels of quality. It also disregarded faculty input on cancellation decisions when all librarians acknowledge that faculty input is decisive. The result was a study of hypothetical preferences, not actual cancellation decisions.[8]

A less hypothetical study was commissioned by publishers themselves in the same year. From the summary:

> The three most important factors used to determine journals for cancellation, in declining order of importance, are that the faculty no longer require it . . . , usage and price. Next, availability of the content via open access (OA) archives and availability via aggregators were ranked equal fourth, but some way behind the first three factors. The journal's impact factor and availability via delayed OA were ranked relatively unimportant. . . . With regard to OA archives, there was a great deal of support for the idea that they would not directly impact journal subscriptions.[9]

In short, toll-access journals have more to fear from their own price increases than from rising levels of green OA. Publishers who keep raising their prices aggravate the access problem for researchers and aggravate the sustainability problem for themselves. If the same publishers blame green OA and lobby against green OA policies, then they obstruct the solution for researchers and do very little to improve their own sustainability.

8. OA may increase submissions and subscriptions.

Some subscription journals have found that OA after an embargo period, even a very short one like two months, actually increases submissions and subscriptions. For example, this was the experience of the American Society for Cell Biology and its journal, *Molecular Biology of the Cell*.

Medknow saw its submissions and subscriptions increase when it began offering unembargoed full-text editions of its journals alongside its toll-access print journals.[10] Hindawi Publishing saw its submissions rise steadily after it converted all its peer-reviewed journals to OA in 2007. Looking back on several years of rapidly growing submissions, company founder and CEO Ahmed Hindawi said in January 2010, "It is clear now more than ever that our open access conversion . . . was the best management decision we have taken. . . ."[11]

9. Some publishers fear that green OA will increase pressure to convert to gold OA.

Some publishers fear that rising levels of green OA will not only trigger toll-access journal cancellations but also increase pressure to convert to gold OA. (Likewise, some OA activists hope for this outcome.)

There are two responses to this two-fold fear. The fear of toll-access cancellations disregards the relevant evidence in points 1–8 above. The fear of conversion to gold OA also disregards relevant evidence, such as Ahmed Hindawi's testimony above, and the testimony of Springer CEO Derk Haank. In 2008 when Springer bought BioMed Central and became the world's largest OA publisher, Haank said: "[W]e see open access publishing as a sustainable part of STM publishing, and not an ideological crusade." (Also see chapter 7 on economics.)[12]

Publishers inexperienced with gold OA needn't defer to publishers with more experience, but they should at least study them.

In fact, OA publishing might be more sustainable than TA publishing, as toll-access prices and the volume of research both grow faster than library budgets. (See section 2.1 on problems.) If publishers acknowledge that gold OA can be sustainable, and even profitable, and merely wish to avoid making lower margins than they make today, then their objection takes on a very different color. They're not at risk of insolvency, just reduced profits, and they're not asserting a need for self-protection, just an entitlement to current levels of profit. There's no reason for public funding agencies acting in the public interest, or private funders acting for charitable purposes, to compromise their missions in order to satisfy that sense of publisher entitlement.

10. Green OA policies are justified even if they do create risks for toll-access journals.

If we're only interested in the effect of rising levels of green OA on toll-access publishers, then we can stop at points 1–9. But if we're interested in good policy, then we must add one more factor: Even if green OA does eventually threaten toll-access journal subscriptions, green OA policies are still justified.

I won't elaborate this point here, since it takes us beyond the topic of casualties to the full case for OA, which is spread throughout the rest of the book. But here's one way to put the debate in perspective: There are good reasons to want to know whether rising levels of green OA will trigger cancellations of toll-access journals, and perhaps even to modify our policies in light of what we learn. But there are no good reasons to put the thriving of incumbent toll-access journals and publishers ahead of the thriving of research itself.

FUTURE

The basic idea of OA is simple.[1] But it has acquired crucial refinements over the years to answer objections and make implementation fast, easy, inexpensive, and lawful. This creates a tension. Because the basic idea is simple, it's continually being rediscovered. However, people fresh to the concept haven't yet absorbed the refinements that answer objections and make implementation fast, easy, inexpensive, and lawful.

Hence, one transition complexity is the fresh convert who supports OA in theory but doesn't understand how to pay for it, how to support peer review, how to avoid copyright infringement, how to avoid violating academic freedom, or how to answer many other long-answered objections and misunderstandings. A kindred complexity is the fresh convert who thinks the whole point is to bypass peer review and convert scholarly communication to blogging and Wikipedia entries, or who thinks the whole point is to disregard copyright in the name of a higher good.

In short, one obstacle is an ironic side-effect of success. This simple idea is spreading faster than its refined elaboration, and it's recruiting allies who repeat old misunderstandings or overlook the strongest answers to frequently asked questions. Fortunately, the net benefits of persuaded newcomers far outweigh the ironic costs.

Scholars who grew up with the internet are steadily replacing those who grew up without it. Scholars who expect to put everything they write online, who expect to find everything they need online, and who expect unlocked content that they may read, search, link, copy, cut/paste, crawl, print, and redistribute, are replacing those who never expected these boons and got used to them, if at all, looking over their shoulder for the copyright police. Scholars who expect to find the very best literature online, harmlessly cohabiting with crap, are inexorably replacing scholars who, despite themselves perhaps, still associate everything online with crap.

Some lazy scholars believe that if something is not free online, then it's not worth reading. This has never been true. However, it's gradually becoming true, and those who want it to become true can accelerate the process. Those who want to live in a world where all peer-reviewed journal literature is free online are themselves growing in numbers and will soon hold power in universities, libraries, learned societies, publishers, funding agencies, and governments. Generational change is on the side of OA.[2]

Even the passage of time without generational change is on the side of OA. Time itself has reduced panic-induced misunderstandings of OA. Everyone is getting used to the ideas that OA literature can be copyrighted, that rights-holders can waive rights and choose open licenses, that OA literature can be peer-reviewed, that the expenses for producing OA literature can be recovered, and that OA and toll-access can coexist even for the same work. Surprisingly many of the early obstacles to OA can be traced to a failure of imagination. Many seasoned academics just couldn't see these possibilities. The problem was not incoherent ideas or stupid people—though both hypotheses circulated widely—but panic, unfamiliarity, and the violation of unquestioned assumptions. For some stakeholders, clear explanations, repetition, or experience with working examples solved the problem. But for others it just took time.[3]

When newcomers misunderstood OA in the past, sometimes they had been misled by an explicit error published somewhere, perhaps by another newcomer. Most of the time, though, they just made unconscious assumptions based on incomplete information and old models. This is the shock of the new at work. If OA uses the internet, then it must bypass peer review. (Right?) If OA articles can be copied ad lib, then there must be copyright problems. (Right?) If OA is free of charge for end-users, then its proponents must be claiming that it costs nothing to produce. (Right?) If it has costs, then recovering those costs must be impossible. (Right?) These conclusions, of course, were uninformed leaps. Many who understood the conventional model (priced, printed, peer-reviewed, copyrighted) saw a proposal for something different and didn't know how many parameters of the old paradigm the new proposal wanted to tweak. The very common, hasty, and incorrect surmise: all of them. It was a classic case of seeing black and white before seeing shades of gray.

Suddenly, everything good about the present system had to be defended, as if it were under attack. A lot of energy was wasted defending peer review, when it was never under attack. Much energy was also wasted defending copyright—or celebrating its demise—when it was never under attack. (More precisely, copyright and copyright excesses were under attack from other directions, but OA itself was always compatible with unrevised, unbalanced, unreconstructed copyright.) The debate about OA often drifted toward the larger debate about what was functional and dysfunctional in the present system of scholarly communication. This was valuable, but mixing narrow OA issues with broader ones created false impressions about what OA really was, how compatible it was with good features of the present system, and how easy it was to implement.

As time passes, we see a steady rise in the proportion of correct to incorrect formulations of OA in high-profile discussions. When people encounter a fragmentary version of the idea for the first time today, their guesswork to flesh it out is guided by a much more reliable range of clues than just a few years ago. If they take the time to run an online search, the chance that they'll find reliable information before someone else's guesswork is approaching 100 percent.

It's tempting to focus on the elegance of OA as a solution to serious problems and overlook the need for the sheer passage of time to overcome the shock of the new. Even if we acknowledge the need for cultural change in the transition to OA—far more critical than technological change—it's easy to underestimate the cultural barriers and the time required to work through them. OA may be compatible with copyright, peer review, profit, print, prestige, and preservation. But that doesn't quiet resistance when those facts about it are precisely the ones hidden by confident false assumptions.

Not all resistance to OA is, or was, based on a misunderstanding of the idea itself. But the largest single portion of it was. That portion is in decline, and that decline has many causes, including the hard work of thousands of people in every discipline and country. But a large and unquestionable part of that decline is due to the passage of time and the rise in mere familiarity with a once-new idea.

The first irony of our still-short history is that OA has been impeded by the turbulence of its own success. The changes wrought by the mere passage of time point up a sad second irony. Nobody is surprised when cultural inertia slows the adoption of radical ideas. But cultural inertia slowed the adoption of OA by leading many people to mistake it for a more radical idea than it actually is.

SELF-HELP

10.1 How to Make Your Work Gold OA

Publishing in an OA journal is like publishing in a conventional journal. Find a suitable journal and submit your manuscript. If you're not familiar with the range of peer-reviewed OA journals, the Directory of Open Access Journals (DOAJ) lets you browse by field. If you don't find an OA journal that meets your standards, check again when you've written your next paper. Things are changing quickly.[1]

If you find an OA journal high in quality but too new to be high in prestige, consider submitting good work there anyway, to help it earn prestige in proportion to its quality. Without this kind of help, especially from senior scholars who have prestige to lend and don't need tenure, good new OA journals can be trapped in a vicious circle, needing high-quality submissions to generate prestige and needing prestige to attract high-quality submissions. (This may be the chief obstacle facing new journals.)

Remember that about 30 percent of OA journals charge author-side fees and about half the articles published in OA journals appear in those fee-based journals. Hence, the best OA journal for your work may charge a publication fee. If so, don't be dismayed or give up on gold OA. Only 12 percent of authors at fee-based OA journals end up paying publication fees out of pocket. For most authors at fee-based journals, the fees are paid by a sponsor, such as a funder or employer, or the fees are waived or discounted by the journal. Moreover, the existence of a fee doesn't mean the journal is engaged in vanity publishing. Your work will be subject to peer review, the fee only kicks in if your work is accepted, and the editors and referees who review it will not know whether you requested a fee waiver. (See sections 5.1 on peer review and chapter 7 on economics.)

If your research was funded, see whether your funder will cover the fee, either by allowing you to pay it with grant funds or by offering auxiliary funds specifically for this purpose. If your research wasn't funded, or if your funder won't cover the fees, check the Open Access Directory or ask a librarian to see whether your institution has a fund to cover OA journal fees. If not, request a fee waiver from the journal.[2]

If you can't pay the fee or get it paid on your behalf, and you don't like the no-fee journals that may exist in your field, don't give up on OA. Just move on to green OA (section 10.2).

Finally, remember that most OA journals are new, and that a new journal can be first-rate without yet having a reputation for being first-rate. To start assessing the quality of a new journal, first see whether you or your colleagues recognize the names of any editors or members of the editorial board. Are they respected scholars? To make a start at assessing honesty and professionalism of a new journal, as opposed to its quality, see whether its publisher belongs to the Open Access Scholarly Publishers Association (OASPA), which has a good code of conduct for members. Many excellent OA publishers don't yet belong to OASPA. But if you're in doubt, you can't go wrong by limiting yourself to OASPA members.[3]

10.2 How to Make Your Work Green OA

If you publish in a toll-access journal, the journal will usually allow you to deposit your peer-reviewed manuscript in an OA repository. To know for sure, read the journal's publication agreement. If your eyes glaze over, or if you want to scan many different publisher policies quickly, see the SHERPA database of publisher policies.[4]

When a journal's standard publishing contract doesn't give you what you need, such as permission to deposit in an OA repository, there are two reasons to ask for modifications. First, you may get what you want. Many publishers who don't give blanket permission for green OA will agree to case-by-case requests. Some publishers, even among the giants where you have the least bargaining power, will pull a "Plan B" agreement from a drawer when authors ask. Second, even when you don't get what you want, you will help educate publishers about shifting demand and rising expectations. This needn't be adversarial. Journals want to know what authors want. In any case, there's no harm in asking. A journal may decline your request, but it will not reject your already-accepted article just because you asked for a more favorable contract.

If you don't know which modifications to request, use an author addendum: a proposed contract revision, written by OA-friendly lawyers, for authors to sign and staple to their standard contract. If a publisher rejects your requested changes or addendum, then consider another publisher.[5]

Don't let all these details about contract modifications scare you off. Most toll-access journals and publishers allow green OA without any contract modifications. I include these details for the minority of cases. Moreover, well-drafted OA policies at funding agencies or universities can ensure permission for green OA without any negotiation between authors and publishers. That's another reason to work toward a good policy at your university. (See chapter 4 on policies.)

If you have permission to deposit your work in an OA repository, then you'll need an OA repository where you have deposit rights. First look for an OA repository in your institution or field.[6] If there aren't any, check again when you've written your next paper. Things are changing fast. In the meantime, consider one of the universal repositories open to research articles of all kinds. I recommend OpenDepot, OpenAire, Academia, and Mendeley.[7]

Consider providing green OA to your preprints or unrefereed manuscripts, not just to your postprints or peer-reviewed articles. One advantage is that you won't need any permission but your own. Because preprints are unpublished, you haven't transferred any rights to a publisher. One disadvantage is that some journals—apparently a shrinking minority but still sizeable in some fields, such as medicine—follow the so-called Ingelfinger Rule and don't accept articles that have already circulated as preprints. If you're worried about this, check with the journals where you'd like to publish and see whether they follow this practice.

Provide OA to your datasets as soon as you can with the fewest restrictions you can. Most repositories accept arbitrary filetypes and could accept data files. But for datasets, repositories optimized for texts are not always as useful as repositories optimized for data. Check out the dedicated data repositories in your field.[8]

Graduate students should provide green OA to their theses and dissertations. Some repositories specialize in theses and dissertations, but most "regular" repositories will also accept them even when the institution doesn't mandate OA for them. (See section 5.2 on OA for theses and dissertations.)

Your top priority should be OA for new and future work. But, time permitting, try to provide green OA to your past publications as well. Sometimes this will mean requesting permissions you didn't obtain at the time, or checking a publisher's current policy on repository deposits. Sometimes it will mean digitizing print-only publications. It may mean putting your hands on the version you are allowed to deposit, for example, the version approved by peer review but prior to copyediting. Your university may be able to offer help with some of these tasks; check with your library.

GLOSSARY

Gold OA
OA through journals, regardless of the journal's business model. *Also see* Green OA.

Gratis OA
Access that is free of charge but not necessarily free of copyright and licensing restrictions. *Also see* Libre OA.

Green OA
OA through repositories. *Also see* Gold OA; Repository; Self-archiving.

Libre OA
Access that is both free of charge (gratis OA) and free of at least some copyright and licensing restrictions. Because there are many possible copyright and licensing restrictions, libre OA is not just one access model but a range of access models. All the degrees of libre OA are alike in permitting uses that exceed fair use (or the local equivalent). *Also see* Gratis OA; License.

License
A statement from a copyright holder telling users what they may and may not do with a copyrighted work. *Open* licenses, such as those from Creative Commons, permit different degrees of libre OA. In the absence of an open license, a copyrighted work is under an all-rights-reserved copyright, its users may not exceed fair use (or the local equivalent), and OA is at most gratis OA. *Also see* Gratis OA; Libre OA.

Open access (OA)
Barrier-free access to online works and other resources. OA literature is digital, online, free of charge (gratis OA), and free of needless copyright and licensing restrictions (libre OA). The term was introduced by the Budapest Open Access Initiative in February 2002.

Publication fee
Sometimes called a processing fee and sometimes (erroneously) an author fee. A fee charged by some OA journals when accepting an article for publication, in order to cover the costs of production. It's one way to cover production costs without charging readers and erecting access barriers. While the bill goes to the author, the fee is usually paid by the author's funder or employer, not by the author out of pocket.

Repository
In the world of OA, a repository is an online database of OA works. Repositories don't perform their own peer-review, but they may host articles peer-reviewed elsewhere. In addition, they frequently host unrefereed preprints, electronic theses and dissertations, books or book chapters, datasets, and digitized print works from the institution's library. *Institutional* repositories aim to host the research output of an institution, while *disciplinary* or *central* repositories aim to host the research output of a field.

Self-archiving
Also called OA archiving. The practice of making work OA by depositing it in an OA repository. *Also see* Green OA.

Toll access (TA)
Access limited to those who pay. The most generic term for the opposite of OA.

Preface

1. See the continually updated bibliography of my articles on open access.
http://www.earlham.edu/~peters/fos/oawritings.htm
Also see Charles W. Bailey Jr., "Transforming Scholarly Publishing through Open Access: A Bibliography," Digital Scholarship, 2010.
http://digital-scholarship.org/tsp/w/tsp.html

Chapter 1

1. Budapest Open Access Initiative, February 14, 2002 (disclosure: I was the principal drafter).
http://www.soros.org/openaccess
Bethesda Statement on Open Access Publishing, June 20, 2003.
http://dash.harvard.edu/bitstream/handle/1/4725199/suber
_bethesda.htm?sequence=1
Berlin Declaration on Open Access to Knowledge in the Sciences and Humanities, October 22, 2003.
http://oa.mpg.de/lang/en-uk/berlin-prozess/berliner-erklarung

2. On the growth of OA over the past decade, see my annual reviews of OA progress, starting in 2003:
http://dash.harvard.edu/bitstream/handle/1/4736588/suber_oa2010
.htm?sequence=1
http://dash.harvard.edu/bitstream/handle/1/4322584/suber_oa2009
.html?sequence=1
http://dash.harvard.edu/bitstream/handle/1/4322588/suber_oa2008
.html?sequence=1
http://dash.harvard.edu/bitstream/handle/1/4322582/suber_oa2007
.html?sequence=1
http://dash.harvard.edu/bitstream/handle/1/4729246/suber_oa2006
.htm?sequence=1
http://dash.harvard.edu/bitstream/handle/1/4729244/suber_oa2005
.htm?sequence=1
http://dash.harvard.edu/bitstream/handle/1/4729243/suber_oa2004
.htm?sequence=1

http://dash.harvard.edu/bitstream/handle/1/4729242/suber_oa2003
.htm?sequence=1

3. This section borrows from several of my previous publications:
"Open Access Overview."

http://dash.harvard.edu/bitstream/handle/1/4729737/suber
_oaoverview.htm?sequence=1

"Creating an Intellectual Commons through Open Access," in Charlotte Hess
and Elinor Ostrom (eds.), *Understanding Knowledge as a Commons: From Theory
to Practice*, MIT Press, 2006.

http://dash.harvard.edu/bitstream/handle/1/4552055/suber
_intellectcommons.pdf?sequence=1

"Six things that researchers need to know about open access," *SPARC Open Access Newsletter*, February 2, 2006.

http://dash.harvard.edu/bitstream/handle/1/4739013/suber
_sixresearchers.htm?sequence=1

My answers to Richard Poynder's interview questions in "The Basement Interviews: Peter Suber," October 19, 2007.

http://poynder.blogspot.com/2007/10/basement-interviews
-peter-suber.html

4. On the origin of scholarly journals, see Jean-Claude Guédon, "In Oldenburg's Long Shadow: Librarians, Research Scientists, Publishers, and the Control of Scientific Publishing," Association of Research Libraries, 2001.

http://www.arl.org/resources/pubs/mmproceedings/138guedon.shtml

Some authors are paid for journal articles. On some of these exceptions, see:
"Open access when authors are paid," *SPARC Open Access Newsletter*, December 2, 2003.

http://dash.harvard.edu/bitstream/handle/1/4552040/suber_paid
.htm?sequence=1

Also see Jufang Shao and Huiyun Shen, "The Outflow of Academic Papers from China," *Learned Publishing* 24, no. 2 (April 2011).

http://dx.doi.org/10.1087/20110203

5. For more, see "Open access, markets, and missions," *SPARC Open Access Newsletter*, March 2, 2010.

http://dash.harvard.edu/bitstream/handle/1/4322590/suber
_oamarkets.html?sequence=1

6. See Steve Hitchcock, "The Effect of Open Access and Downloads ('Hits') on Citation Impact: A Bibliography of Studies," the Open Citation Project, continually updated.

http://opcit.eprints.org/oacitation-biblio.html

Also see Alma Swan's technical report, which includes summary findings of all the major studies from 2001 to 2010:

"Open Access Citation Advantage: Studies and Results to Date," Technical Report, School of Electronics & Computer Science, University of Southampton, August 2010.

http://eprints.ecs.soton.ac.uk/18516

Also see Ben Wagner's "Open Access Citation Advantage: An Annotated Bibliography," *Issues in Science and Technology Librarianship*, Winter 2010.

http://www.istl.org/10-winter/article2.html

Excerpt:

> Though [the explanation for the correlation] is not settled, the bibliography cites a number of studies designed to test the hypothesis of confounding extraneous causes. It is clear that open access articles are downloaded far more than toll access articles. Studies indicate this download advantage is easily 100% over toll access articles. It seems unlikely such a large download advantage would not to some degree eventually influence the number of citations. . . . Publication in an open access journal (Gold OA) apparently is not required to get a significant OA citation advantage.

Among the continuing controversies is how far to attribute the correlation to self-selection, or decisions by authors to deposit their best work in OA repositories. Tending to deny the OA citation advantage, a December 2010 study by Philip Davis tried to rule out self-selection bias by randomly making some articles OA and others toll access. The OA articles were downloaded more often but not cited more often than the toll-access articles. Tending to confirm the OA citation advantage, an October 2010 study by Yassine Gargouri, Stevan Harnad, and colleagues tried to rule out self-selection bias by showing that the OA citation advantage was just as high for mandated OA archiving as it was for voluntary OA archiving. See Philip M. Davis, "Does Open Access Lead to Increased Readership and Citations? A Randomized Controlled Trial of Articles Published in APS [American Physiological Society] Journals," *The Physiologist*, 53 (6), December 2010.

http://www.the-aps.org/publications/tphys/2010html/December/open_access.htm

Also see Yassine Gargouri et al., "Self-Selected or Mandated, Open Access Increases Citation Impact for Higher Quality Research," *PLoS ONE* [Public Library of Science], October 18, 2010.

http://dx.doi.org/10.1371/journal.pone.0013636

7. See Harnad's use of this analogy in this March 2007 discussion thread from the American Scientist Open Access Forum.

http://users.ecs.soton.ac.uk/harnad/Hypermail/Amsci/6199.html

8. Tim O'Reilly, "Piracy is Progressive Taxation, and Other Thoughts on the Evolution of Online Distribution," *O'Reilly P2P*, December 11, 2002.

http://openp2p.com/lpt/a/3015

9. Budapest Open Access Initiative, February 14, 2002.

http://www.soros.org/openaccess/read.shtml

10. This section borrows from two of my previous publications: "Open Access Overview."

http://dash.harvard.edu/bitstream/handle/1/4729737/suber
_oaoverview.htm?sequence=1

"A field guide to misunderstandings about open access," *SPARC Open Access Newsletter*, April 2, 2009.

http://dash.harvard.edu/bitstream/handle/1/4322571/suber
_fieldguide.html?sequence=1

11. This section borrows from two of my previous publications: "Open access and quality," *SPARC Open Access Newsletter*, October 2, 2006.

http://dash.harvard.edu/bitstream/handle/1/4552042/suber
_oaquality.htm?sequence=1

"Balancing author and publisher rights," *SPARC Open Access Newsletter*, June 2, 2007.

http://dash.harvard.edu/bitstream/handle/1/4391158/suber
_balancing.htm?sequence=1

12. In a December 2010 speech, Neelie Kroes, Vice-President of the European Commission for the Digital Agenda, remarked that "the beauty of open access is that it is not against anybody. It is for the free movement of knowledge."

http://europa.eu/rapid/pressReleasesAction.do?reference=SPEECH/10
/716&format=HTML&aged=0&language=EN&guiLanguage=en

Chapter 2

1. This section borrows from several of my previous publications: "Removing the Barriers to Research: An Introduction to Open Access for Librarians," *College & Research Libraries News*, 64 (February 2003), pp. 92–94, 113.

http://dash.harvard.edu/bitstream/handle/1/3715477/suber_crln
.html?sequence=5

"The scaling argument," *SPARC Open Access Newsletter*, March 2, 2004.
http://dash.harvard.edu/bitstream/handle/1/4723859/suber_scaling
.htm?sequence=1

"Problems and opportunities (blizzards and beauty)," *SPARC Open Access Newl-setter*, July 2, 2007.
http://dash.harvard.edu/bitstream/handle/1/4727450/suber_problem
sopps.htm?sequence=1

"A bill to overturn the NIH policy," *SPARC Open Access Newsletter*, October 2, 2008.
http://dash.harvard.edu/bitstream/handle/1/4322592/suber_nihbill
.html?sequence=1

2. For the two decades, from the mid-1980s to the mid-2000s, the price of toll-access journals rose more than 2.5 times faster than inflation. Association for Research Libraries, *Monograph and Serial Expenditures in ARL Libraries, 1986–2004*.
http://www.arl.org/bm~doc/monser04.pdf
In June 2010, Mark Bauerlein and four co-authors reported that "[f]rom 1978 to 2001, libraries at the University of California at Los Angeles . . . saw their subscription costs alone climb by 1,300 percent."
http://chronicle.com/article/We-Must-Stop-the-Avalanche-of/65890
Between 1986 and 1999, "serial costs increased at 9% a year [while] library materials budgets increased at only 6.7% a year." During the same period, the unit price of journals increased by 207%, while the cost of health care increased by only 107%. See the Scholarly Communication FAQ from the University of California's Office of Systemwide Library Planning, February 29, 2003.
http://www.ucop.edu/copyright/2003-02-27/faq.html
For prices of individual journals, see MIT's Expensive Journals List: Current MIT subscriptions costing more than $5,000/year (last updated 7/16/09).
http://web.archive.org/web/20101030035020/http://libraries.mit.edu
/about/scholarly/expensive-titles.html
For the latest survey of journal prices and the average prices by field, see Stephen Bosch, Kittie Henderson, & Heather Klusendorf, "Periodicals Price Survey 2011: Under Pressure, Times Are Changing," *Library Journal*, April 14, 2011. It shows journal prices continuing to rise faster than inflation, and library serials budgets actually declining, not merely growing more slowly than inflation.
http://www.libraryjournal.com/lj/home/890009-264/periodicals_price
_survey_2011_under.html.csp

3. Directory of Open Access Journals.

    http://www.doaj.org

Most observers estimate that there are about 25,000 peer-reviewed journals in all fields and languages, making the OA portion about 26 percent of the total. There's some evidence that the average OA journal publishes fewer articles/year than the average toll-access journal, making the OA portion (by articles rather than journals) even smaller than 26 percent. If we supplement the number of peer-reviewed articles published by OA journals with the number of peer-reviewed OA articles published by toll-access journals but disseminated with permission by OA repositories, the portion goes up again.

4. "Overcoming Barriers: Access to Research Information Content," Research Information Network, December 2009.

    http://www.rin.ac.uk/our-work/using-and-accessing-information
    -resources/overcoming-barriers-access-research-information

5. See Robin Peek, "Harvard Faculty Mandates OA," *Information Today*, April 1, 2008.

    http://www.allbusiness.com/legal/contracts-law-licensing-agree
    ments/8957081-1.html

Here's the full quotation from Stuart Shieber: "At Harvard, serials duplication has been all but eliminated and serious cancellation efforts have been initiated. Monograph collecting has been substantially affected as well. In total, our faculty have seen qualitative reductions in access to the literature."

    http://dash.harvard.edu/bitstream/handle/1/4322590/suber
    _oamarkets.html?sequence=1

The Harvard University library is the largest academic library in the world and has the largest annual budget. But see "Libraries on the Edge," *Harvard Magazine*, Jan–Feb 2010: "[B]udgetary pressures that have been building during the past decade, and intensified in the past year, threaten the ability of the world's largest private library to collect works as broadly as it has in the past. . . ." Library Directory Robert Darnton said acquisitions fell "precipitously" the previous year and described the situation as "a crisis."

    http://harvardmagazine.com/2010/01/harvard-libraries-under
    -pressure

6. The numbers I quote are based on personal communications with librarians. Unfortunately it's hard to get data on subscriptions to peer-reviewed journals alone rather than subscriptions to the larger category of serials.

7. As a result of bundling, the number of titles to which academic libraries in North America subscribed rose by 42 percent in the from the mid-1980s to

the mid-2000s, but library expenditures for those titles rose by 273 percent or nearly four times faster than inflation. Association for Research Libraries, *Monograph and Serial Expenditures in ARL Libraries, 1986–2004*.

http://www.arl.org/bm~doc/monser04.pdf

Also see Kittie S. Henderson and Stephen Bosch, "Seeking the New Normal: Periodicals Price Survey 2010," *Library Journal*, April 15, 2010: "Libraries are aware . . . that the top journals in a bundle continue to generate the majority of use while the low-use journals still account for a large portion of the cost."

http://www.libraryjournal.com/article/CA6725256.html

In November 2010, the Research Libraries UK announced that "it would not support future journal big deals unless they showed real price reductions."

http://www.rluk.ac.uk/content/rluk-calls-journal-pricing-restraint

8. See Elsevier's financial summary for 2010. On revenues of £2,026 million (about $3,290 million), it earned profits of £724 million (about $1,180 million), or 36 percent.

http://reports.reedelsevier.com/ar10/business_review/financial
_summary.htm

In 2010, ExxonMobil earned revenues of $383,221 million and profits of $107,827 million, or 28.1 percent.

http://moneycentral.msn.com/investor/invsub/results/statemnt
.aspx?symbol=us%3AXOM

Journal publishing is more profitable at Elsevier than entertainment is at Disney (17.7 percent).

http://moneycentral.msn.com/investor/invsub/results/statemnt
.aspx?symbol=DIS

9. See the Big Deal Contract Project from Ted Bergstrom, Paul Courant, and Preston McAfee.

http://www.econ.ucsb.edu/~tedb/Journals/BundleContracts.html

For details on Elsevier's attempt to block the release of its big-deal contract with Washington State, see the June 2009 press release from the Association Research Libraries (ARL).

http://www.arl.org/news/pr/elsevier-wsu-23jun09.shtml

10. See James McPherson, "A Crisis in Scholarly Publishing," *Perspectives*, October 2003. Also see Association for Research Libraries, *Monograph and Serial Expenditures in ARL Libraries, 1986–2004*.

http://www.arl.org/bm~doc/monser04.pdf

The number of books purchased by the ARL libraries from the mid-1980s to the mid-2000s dropped by nearly 10 percent, and the expenditure for books rose more slowly than the inflation rate.

11. For more on the permissions crisis, see my article "Removing the Barriers to Research: An Introduction to Open Access for Librarians," *College & Research Libraries News*, 64 (February 2003), pp. 92–94, 113.

> http://dash.harvard.edu/bitstream/handle/1/3715477/suber_crln .html?sequence=5

12. In March 2011, the International Association of Scientific, Technical & Medical Publishers estimated that 96 percent of journals in the STM fields had online editions. Of course, most were toll access.

> http://www.stm-assoc.org/2011_04_19_STM_statement_on _licensing_and_authors_rights.pdf

13. In 2008, the Research Information Network calculated that researchers worldwide donate to journal publishers £1.9 billion/year (about $3 billion/ year) in time spent on performing peer review.

> http://www.timeshighereducation.co.uk/story.asp?sectioncode=26&st orycode=402189

14. For more on publisher objections that OA initiatives interfere with the market, see "Will open access undermine peer review?" *SPARC Open Access Newsletter*, September 2, 2007.

> http://dash.harvard.edu/bitstream/handle/1/4322578/suber_peer .html?sequence=1

"Open access, markets, and missions," *SPARC Open Access Newsletter*, March 2, 2010.

> http://dash.harvard.edu/bitstream/handle/1/4322590/suber _oamarkets.html?sequence=1

15. Theodore and Carl Bergstrom have shown that toll-access journal prices are either unrelated to quality or inversely related to it. Their analysis shows that "libraries typically must pay 4 to 6 times as much per page for journals owned by commercial publishers as for journals owned by non-profit societies. These differences in price do not reflect differences in the quality of the journals. In fact the commercial journals are on average less cited than the non-profits and the average cost per citation of commercial journals ranges from 5 to 15 times as high as that of their non-profit counterparts." See Theodore and Carl Bergstrom, "Can 'author pays' journals compete with 'reader pays'?" *Nature*, May 20, 2004.

> http://www.nature.com/nature/focus/accessdebate/22.html

Theodore Bergstrom and Preston McAfee maintain the Journal Cost Effectiveness calculator, which computes the cost per article and cost per citation for a given journal.

http://www.journalprices.com

For a summary of their data, showing that for-profit publishers charge more per article and per citation, see their statistical summary from April 2011.

http://www.mcafee.cc/Journal/Summary.pdf

http://www.mcafee.cc/Journal/explanation2010.html

On quality, in 2005 Sally Morris summarized the studies to date: "All the evidence shows that non-profit journals are on average both less expensive and of higher quality. . . ." See Sally Morris, "The true costs of scholarly journal publishing," *Learned Publishing* 18 (2, April 2005), 115–126.

http://www.ingentaselect.com/rpsv/cgi-bin/cgi?ini=xref&body=linker& reqdoi=10.1087/0953151053584975

16. See Roger Clarke, "The cost profiles of alternative approaches to journal publishing," *First Monday*, December 3, 2007.

http://firstmonday.org/htbin/cgiwrap/bin/ojs/index.php/fm/article /view/2048

17. See the Credit Suisse First Boston financial analysis of the STM journal industry, April 6, 2004. This report is not online, but I summarized it in the *SPARC Open Access Newsletter* for May 3, 2004.

http://dash.harvard.edu/bitstream/handle/1/3997172/suber_news73 .html?sequence=2

Toll-access publishers don't dispute this, but they claim that the same economics apply to fee-based OA journals. For five reasons why they don't, see my article, "Open access and quality," SPARC Open Access Newsletter, October 2, 2006.

http://dash.harvard.edu/bitstream/handle/1/4552042/suber _oaquality.htm?sequence=1

18. Jan Velterop, "Institutional Journal Costs in an Open Access Environment," *LibLicense*, April 26, 2006.

http://www.library.yale.edu/~llicense/ListArchives/0604/msg00117 .html

On the on the moral hazard, see Stuart Shieber's article-length blog posts from March 1, 2011, and July 31, 2010.

http://blogs.law.harvard.edu/pamphlet/2011/03/01/institutional -memberships-for-open-access-publishers-considered-harmful
http://blogs.law.harvard.edu/pamphlet/2010/07/31/will-open -access-publication-fees-grow-out-of-control

19. While all OA initiatives help researchers, only some help libraries by reducing prices or enabling cancellations. For more, see "Helping scholars and helping libraries," *SPARC Open Access Newsletter*, April 2, 2005.

> http://dash.harvard.edu/bitstream/handle/1/4552051/suber_helping
> .htm?sequence=1

20. I first used the Croesus example in an interview with Richard Poynder, "Suber: Leader of a Leaderless Revolution," *Information Today*, July 1, 2011.

> http://www.infotoday.com/it/jul11/Suber-Leader-of-a-Leaderless
> -Revolution.shtml

Also see "The scaling argument," *SPARC Open Access Newsletter*, March 2, 2004.
> http://dash.harvard.edu/bitstream/handle/1/4723859/suber_scaling
> .htm?sequence=1

21. Crispin Davis, "Science books are vanishing from reach," *The Guardian*, February 19, 2005.

> http://education.guardian.co.uk/higher/research/story
> /0,9865,1418097,00.html

The charitable reading of Davis's argument is that he believes the serials crisis is a library budget problem, not a journal pricing problem. This position overlooks that (1) not even the University of Croesus can keep pace with the growing volume of the literature, and (2) no real library anywhere, not even Harvard, has kept pace with decades of hyperinflationary price increases.

22. Lawrence H. Pitts, Chair of University of California Academic Senate, an open letter to the University of California faculty, January 7, 2004.

> http://libraries.universityofcalifornia.edu/news/facmemoschol
> comm_010704.pdf

23. This section borrows from several of my previous publications:
"The scaling argument," *SPARC Open Access Newsletter*, March 2, 2004.
> http://dash.harvard.edu/bitstream/handle/1/4723859/suber_scaling
> .htm?sequence=1

"Problems and opportunities (blizzards and beauty)," *SPARC Open Access Newsletter*, July 2, 2007.

> http://dash.harvard.edu/bitstream/handle/1/4727450/suber_problem
> sopps.htm?sequence=1

"Open access and the last-mile problem for knowledge," *SPARC Open Access Newsletter*, July 2, 2008.

> http://dash.harvard.edu/bitstream/handle/1/4322587/suber_lastmile
> .html?sequence=1

"Open access, markets, and missions," *SPARC Open Access Newsletter*, March 2, 2010.

> http://dash.harvard.edu/bitstream/handle/1/4322590/suber_oamar kets.html?sequence=1

24. See H. A. Washington, ed., *The Writings of Thomas Jefferson*, printed by the United States Congress, 1853–54, vol. VI, 180.

25. At the launch of *PLoS Medicine* in May 2004, Nobel laureate and PLoS co-founder Harold Varmus said, "Thanks to the Internet and new strategies for financing publication costs, it is now possible to share the results of medical research with anyone, anywhere, who could benefit from it. How could we not do it?"

> http://www.library.yale.edu/~llicense/ListArchives/0405/msg00038 .html

Chapter 3

1. This section borrows from several of my previous publications:
"Open Access Overview."

> http://dash.harvard.edu/bitstream/handle/1/4729737/suber_oaover view.htm?sequence=1

"Thinking about prestige, quality, and open access," *SPARC Open Access Newsletter*, September 2, 2008.

> http://dash.harvard.edu/bitstream/handle/1/4322577/suber _oaquality.html?sequence=1

"A field guide to misunderstandings about open access," *SPARC Open Access Newsletter*, April 2, 2009.

> http://dash.harvard.edu/bitstream/handle/1/4322571/suber _fieldguide.html?sequence=1

2. See Marie E. McVeigh, "Open Access Journals in the ISI Citation Databases: Analysis of Impact Factors and Citation Patterns Thomson Scientific," Thomson Scientific, October 2004.

> http://science.thomsonreuters.com/m/pdfs/openaccesscitations2.pdf

3. The first peer-reviewed OA journals were launched in the 1980s. See the list of "Early OA journals" at the Open Access Directory.

> http://oad.simmons.edu/oadwiki/Early_OA_journals

While some OA journals are now fairly old, the average age of OA journals is far lower than the average age of toll-access journals. On the disadvantages that arise from being new, see my article "Thinking about prestige, quality, and open access," *SPARC Open Access Newsletter*, September 2, 2008.

> http://dash.harvard.edu/bitstream/handle/1/4322577/suber
> _oaquality.html?sequence=1

4.   For current data on how many toll-access publishers and journals give blanket permission for green OA, see the SHERPA statistics page.

> http://www.sherpa.ac.uk/romeo/statistics.php

For toll-access journal and publisher policies on green OA, see SHERPA's Rights MEtadata for Open archiving database (RoMEO).

> http://www.sherpa.ac.uk/romeo.php

For evidence that toll-access publishers permitting green OA approach 100 percent when authors are subject to green OA mandates, see the Open Access Directory list of publisher policies on NIH-funded authors.

> http://oad.simmons.edu/oadwiki/Publisher_policies_on_NIH-funded
> _authors

> http://www.arl.org/sparc/media/blog/publishers-accommodate
> -nih-funded-authors.shtml

5. See the Open Archives Initiative.

> http://www.openarchives.org

Also see my article, "The case for OAI in the age of Google," *SPARC Open Access Newsletter*, May 3, 2004.

6. For institutional repositories, see the Registry of Open Access Repositories (ROAR) and the Directory of Open Access Repositories (OpenDOAR).

> http://roar.eprints.org
> http://www.opendoar.org

For disciplinary repositories organized by field, see the wiki-based list at the Open Access Directory.

> http://oad.simmons.edu/oadwiki/Disciplinary_repositories

7. See arXiv.

> http://arxiv.org

See PubMed Central.

> http://www.pubmedcentral.gov

8. See the data collected by Arthur Sale in a series of publications from 2005 and 2006.

> http://fcms.its.utas.edu.au/scieng/comp/project.asp?lProjectId=1830

9. See Muluken Wubayehu Alemayehu, "Researchers' attitude to using institutional repositories: A case study of the Oslo University Institutional Repository," Master's thesis at Oslo University College, 2010. Surveyed authors had "a low level awareness of the Institutional repository" at the same time as "a positive attitude towards providing free access to scholarly research results...."

> https://oda.hio.no/jspui/handle/10642/426

Also see a SURFShare survey of Dutch faculty from the Fall of 2010. "Almost 90% of the lectors ["associate professors who carry out research and organise knowledge networks"] at Dutch universities of applied sciences are in favor of making their research results freely available. . . . They also say they need to know just what Open Access publication actually involves."

> http://www.openaccess.nl/index.php?option=com_content&view=artic
> le&id=232:majority-of-lectors-favour-open-access
> -publication&catid=1:news-archive

For a thorough review of the literature up to 2009, showing low levels of author opposition and high levels of unfamiliarity, see Jenny Fry et al., "PEER Behavioural Research: Authors and Users vis-à-vis Journals and Repositories: Baseline report," PEER Project, September 2009, especially pp. 15–17.

> http://www.peerproject.eu/fileadmin/media/reports/Final_revision
> _-_behavioural_baseline_report_-_20_01_10.pdf

10. This section borrows from two of my previous publications:
"Eleventh hour for SCOAP3," *SPARC Open Access Newsletter*, December 2, 2010.

> http://dash.harvard.edu/bitstream/handle/1/4736587/suber_scoap3
> .htm?sequence=1

My answers to Richard Poynder's interview questions in "The Basement Interviews: Peter Suber," October 19, 2007.

> http://poynder.blogspot.com/2007/10/basement-interviews
> -peter-suber.html

11. I discuss this kind of decoupling in "Eleventh hour for SCOAP3," *SPARC Open Access Newsletter*, December 2, 2010.

> http://dash.harvard.edu/bitstream/handle/1/4736587/suber_scoap3
> .htm?sequence=1

12. This section borrows from several of my previous publications:
"Open Access Overview"

> http://dash.harvard.edu/bitstream/handle/1/4729737/suber
> _oaoverview.htm?sequence=1

My answers to Richard Poynder's interview questions in "The Basement Interviews: Peter Suber," October 19, 2007.

> http://poynder.blogspot.com/2007/10/basement-interviews
> -peter-suber.html

"Gratis and libre open access," *SPARC Open Access Newsletter*, August 2, 2008.
> http://dash.harvard.edu/bitstream/handle/1/4322580/suber_oagratis
> .html?sequence=1

"Open access policy options for funding agencies and universities," *SPARC Open Access Newsletter*, February 2, 2009.

> http://dash.harvard.edu/bitstream/handle/1/4322589/suber
> _oaoptions.html?sequence=1

"Ten challenges for open-access journals," *SPARC Open Access Newsletter*, October 2, 2009.

> http://dash.harvard.edu/bitstream/handle/1/4316131
> /suber_10challenges.html?sequence=2

13. For the fair use section of the U.S. copyright statute, see 17 USC 107. The statute makes the boundary between fair and unfair use slightly less fuzzy by listing four factors for determining whether a use is fair. But all four factors have their own fuzz, and it's very hard to know how they will be weighed in a given case without going to court.

> http://www.copyright.gov/title17

14. For the distinction in the world of software, see the Wikipedia article "Gratis versus libre."

> http://en.wikipedia.org/wiki/Gratis_versus_Libre

15. For detail on how these two distinctions intersect, see the table I posted to *Open Access News*, August 2, 2008.

> http://www.earlham.edu/~peters/fos/2008/08/greengold-oa-and
> -gratislibre-oa.html

16. See Creative Commons.
> http://creativecommons.org

17. The public domain is one way to solve the permission problem for OA. But if public-domain works are not yet digital and online, they are not yet OA. This is a nontrivial gap, and around the world institutions and governments are devoting enormous amounts of money and energy to digitizing works in the public domain in order to put them online and make them OA.

18. Open Access Scholarly Publishers Association (OASPA).
    http://www.oaspa.org
SPARC Europe Seal of Approval program for OA journals.
    https://mx2.arl.org/Lists/SPARC-OAForum/Message/4329.html
    http://www.doaj.org/doaj?func=loadTempl&templ=faq#seal

19. For details on the long, difficult struggle to enact and strengthen the gratis OA policy at the NIH, see my eighteen articles on the process from 2004 to 2009.
    https://mx2.arl.org/Lists/SPARC-OAForum/Message/5637.html
For university OA policies adopted by unanimous faculty votes, see the list of unanimous faculty votes at the Open Access Directory.
    http://oad.simmons.edu/oadwiki/Unanimous_faculty_votes

20. As of May 12, 2011: 1,370 out of 6,497 journals in the DOAJ, or 21.1 percent, use some kind of CC license.
    http://www.doaj.org/?func=licensedJournals
As of the same date, 723 (11.1 percent) have the SPARC Europe Seal of Approval (requiring CC-BY).
    http://www.doaj.org/?func=sealedJournals
The DOAJ doesn't actually count journals with CC-BY licenses. It counts journals with the SPARC Europe Seal, which requires CC-BY licenses. But the seal also requires journals to share metadata in a certain way. Hence, it's possible for many journals to use CC-BY and fail to earn the seal because they don't share their metadata appropriately. In that case the SPARC Seal tally would undercount the journals using CC-BY. But in fact, many more DOAJ journals share their metadata than use CC-BY, making the seal tally a good approximation to a CC-BY tally. Thanks to Lars Björnshauge for the latter detail.

21. See "Clipping Our Own Wings Copyright and Creativity in Communication Research," a report from the Ad Hoc Committee on Fair Use and Academic Freedom, International Communication Association, March 2010. A survey of scholars in the field of communications found that a third avoided topics raising copyright issues, a fifth faced publisher resistance to scholarly use of copyrighted work, and a fifth abandoned research in progress because of copyright problems. Many are told to obtain permission to discuss or criticize copyrighted works.
    http://www.centerforsocialmedia.org/fair-use/related-materials
    /documents/clipping-our-own-wings-copyright-and-creativity
    -communication-r

Chapter 4

1. This section borrows from several of my previous publications:
"Open access policy options for funding agencies and universities," *SPARC Open Access Newsletter*, February 2, 2009.

> http://dash.harvard.edu/bitstream/handle/1/4322589/suber
> _oaoptions.html?sequence=1

"Three principles for university open access policies," *SPARC Open Access Newsletter*, April 2, 2008.

> http://dash.harvard.edu/bitstream/handle/1/4317659
> /suber_3principles.html?sequence=2

"The Primacy of Authors in Achieving Open Access," *Nature*, June 10, 2004.

> http://www.nature.com/nature/focus/accessdebate/24.html

"Open access to electronic theses and dissertations (ETDs)," *SPARC Open Access Newsletter*, July 2, 2006.

> http://dash.harvard.edu/bitstream/handle/1/4727443/suber_theses
> .htm?sequence=1

2. The best list of funder and university OA policies is Registry of Open Access Repository Material Archiving Policies (ROARMAP).

> http://roarmap.eprints.org

For case studies of OA policies at universities, see the "oa.case.policies.universities" tag library at the Open Access Tracking Project.

> http://www.connotea.org/tag/oa.case.policies.universities

For case studies of OA policies at funding agencies, see the "oa.case.policies.funders" tag library.

> http://www.connotea.org/tag/oa.case.policies.funders

3. Universities with request or encouragement policies include Germany's University of Bielefeld (June 2005), Canada's University of Athabasca (November 2006), Carnegie Mellon University (November 2007), Swedish University of Agricultural Sciences (February 2008), University of Oregon (February 2008), University of Washington (April 2009), University of Utrecht (April 2009), Finland's University of Tampere (August 2009), University of Virginia (September 2009), the librarians and archivists at York University (October 2009), Italy's University of Sassari (January 2010), San Jose State University (April 2010), the librarians and archivists at Queen's University (April 2010), the librarians at Arizona State University (October 2010), and Emory University (March 2011).

4. See Alma Swan's chart of new green OA mandates from 2002 to 2010.

http://www.openscholarship.org/jcms/c_6226/open-access-policies
-for-universities-and-research-institutions?hlText=policies

Also see the smaller chart on the front page of ROARMAP, automatically up-dated as new policies are registered with ROARMAP.

http://roarmap.eprints.org

On the principle that university policies must respect faculty freedom to sub-mit their work to the journals of their choice, see "Three principles for univer-sity open access policies," *SPARC Open Access Newsletter*, April 2, 2008.

http://dash.harvard.edu/bitstream/handle/1/4317659/suber
_3principles.html?sequence=2

For the same reason that a gold OA mandate would be bad policy today, it's a bad idea to propose a green OA mandate to a population unclear on the green/gold distinction and likely to construe the proposal as a gold OA mandate. See "Lessons from Maryland," *SPARC Open Access Newsletter*, June 2, 2009.

http://dash.harvard.edu/bitstream/handle/1/4322585/suber_mary
land.html?sequence=1

5. Universities with loophole mandates include the University of Zurich (July 2005), Macquarie University (August 2008), University College London (Oc-tober 2008), University of Westminster (July 2009), Edith Cowan University (September 2009), University of Strathclyde (October 2009), Dublin Institute of Technology (December 2009), Brunel University (January 2010), Univer-sity of Ghent (January 2010), Concordia University (April 2010), Karlsruher Institut für Technologie (May 2010), V.N. Karazin Kharkiv National University (August 2010), College of Mount Saint Vincent (October 2010), Malmö Uni-versity (December 2010).

6. The deposit mandate was pioneered by Southampton University's Depart-ment of Electronics and Computer Science, February 5, 2003. It was the first university OA mandate anywhere.

http://roarmap.eprints.org/1

Southampton later adopted a university-wide version of the same type of policy on April 4, 2008.

http://roarmap.eprints.org/8

Stevan Harnad, who favors this model, calls it "immediate deposit / optional access" (IDOA).

http://openaccess.eprints.org/index.php?/archives/71-guid.html

Universities with Southampton-style deposit mandates include Queensland University of Technology (initially September 2003 and strengthened since), University of Minho (initially December 2004 and strengthened since), University of Liège (initially March 2007 and strengthened since), University of Pretoria (May 2009), University of Northern Colorado Libraries (December 2009), University of Salford (January 2010), and University of Hong Kong (April 2010).

7. The Harvard Faculty of Arts and Sciences adopted this policy by a unanimous vote in February 2008.

    http://osc.hul.harvard.edu/hfaspolicy

    http://dash.harvard.edu/bitstream/handle/1/4322574/suber_harvard
    .html?sequence=1

Today, seven of Harvard's nine schools operate under similar policies.

    http://osc.hul.harvard.edu

Universities with rights-retention mandates along the lines of the Harvard Faculty of Arts and Sciences include Harvard University Law School (May 2008), Stanford University School of Education (June 2008), Harvard University Kennedy School of Government (March 2009), Massachusetts Institute of Technology (March 2009), University of Kansas (April 2009), University of Oregon Library Faculty (May 2009), University of Oregon Department of Romance Languages (May 2009), Harvard University Graduate School of Education (June 2009), Trinity University (October 2009), Oberlin College (November 2009), Wake Forest University Library Faculty (February 2010), Harvard University Business School (February 2010), Duke University (March 2010), University of Puerto Rico Law School (March 2010), Harvard University Divinity School (November 2010), the University of Hawaii-Manoa (December 2010), Strathmore University (February 2011), and the Harvard University Graduate School of Design (April 2011).

Also see Simon Frankel and Shannon Nestor, "How Faculty Authors Can Implement an Open Access Policy at Their Institutions," Covington and Burling, August 2010. In a legal analysis commissioned by SPARC and Science Commons, attorneys Frankel and Nestor recommended the rights-retention model used by Harvard and MIT for advancing OA and avoiding copyright pitfalls.

    http://sciencecommons.org/wp-content/uploads/Opening-the
    -Door.pdf

8. The EPrints repository software from Southampton University introduced the email-request button in April 2006. Later the same week, a developer at Minho University released code for adding the feature to DSpace repositories.

    http://www.eprints.org/news/features/request_button.php
    https://mx2.arl.org/Lists/SPARC-OAForum/Message/2931.html

9. The Wellcome Trust OA mandate took effect on October 1, 2005.
    http://www.wellcome.ac.uk/About-us/Policy/Spotlight-issues/Open
    -access/Policy/index.htm
Also see my article on the policy, "The Wellcome Trust OA mandate takes ef-
fect," *SPARC Open Access Newsletter*, October 2, 2005.
    http://dash.harvard.edu/bitstream/handle/1/4723858/suber_wel
    lcometrust.htm?sequence=1
The NIH policy took effect as an encouragement policy on May 2, 2005, and as
a mandate on April 7, 2008.
    http://publicaccess.nih.gov
Also see my eighteen articles on the NIH policy.
    https://mx2.arl.org/Lists/SPARC-OAForum/Message/5637.html
Among other funding agencies with no-waiver rights-retention policies are
the Arthritis Research Campaign, Cancer Research UK, the UK Department
of Health, the Howard Hughes Medical Institute, the UK Medical Research
Council, and the Swedish Research Council.
    In a major report on the state of OA in the United Kingdom, the Centre
for Research Communications recommended that that UK funders "to take a
robust attitude to copyright and reserve copyright for OA archiving prior to
any downstream agreement with publishers." See "Research Communication
Strategy Quarterly Report," July 2010.
    http://ie-repository.jisc.ac.uk/488/2/RCS_quarterly_report_July_2010
    _anonymised.pdf

10. On publisher accommodation of the NIH policy, see the Open Access Directory list of publisher policies on NIH-funded authors.
    http://oad.simmons.edu/oadwiki/Publisher_policies_on_NIH-funded
    _authors
    http://www.arl.org/sparc/media/blog/publishers-accommodate
    -nih-funded-authors.shtml

11. "Open access policy options for funding agencies and universities," *SPARC
Open Access Newsletter*, February 2, 2009.
    http://dash.harvard.edu/bitstream/handle/1/4322589/suber
    _oaoptions.html?sequence=1

12. For my arguments in support of OA mandates for theses and dissertations,
see "Open access to electronic theses and dissertations (ETDs)," *SPARC Open
Access Newsletter*, July 2, 2006.
    http://dash.harvard.edu/bitstream/handle/1/4727443/suber_theses
    .htm?sequence=1

For a list of ETD mandates, see ROARMAP.

 http://roarmap.eprints.org

The first universities in the world to limit the review of journal articles for promotion and tenure to those on deposit in the institutional repository were Napier University (now called Edinburgh Napier University) and the University of Liège, both in 2008. They've since been followed, among others, by China's National Science Library, the University of Oregon Department of Romance Languages, India's International Center for Tropical Agriculture, and Canada's Institute for Research in Construction.

13. This section borrows from several of my previous publications:
"Open access to electronic theses and dissertations (ETDs)," *SPARC Open Access Newsletter*, July 2, 2006.

 http://dash.harvard.edu/bitstream/handle/1/4727443/suber_theses
 .htm?sequence=1

My comments on the word "mandate" in dialog with Jan Velterop, March 4, 2007.

 http://theparachute.blogspot.com/2007/03/mandate-debate
 .html#9025093357099085662

"A field guide to misunderstandings about open access," *SPARC Open Access Newsletter*, April 2, 2009.

 http://dash.harvard.edu/bitstream/handle/1/4322571/suber
 _fieldguide.html?sequence=1

14. See Stuart Shieber on the word "mandate."
 http://blogs.law.harvard.edu/pamphlet/2009/06/30/university-open
 -access-policies-as-mandates

15. Note that many funding agencies deliberately avoid the word "contract" for their funding agreements and prefer to consider them awards or gifts.

16. See Alma Swan and Sheridan Brown, "Authors and open access publishing," *Learned Publishing* 17 (3) 2004, pp. 219–224; and Swan and Brown, "Open access self-archiving: An author study," Departmental Technical Report, 2005.

 http://eprints.ecs.soton.ac.uk/11003

 http://cogprints.org/4385

Also see the summary of Swan and Brown's data at Enabling Open Scholarship.
 http://www.openscholarship.org/jcms/c_6194/researchers-attitudes
 -towards-mandatory-open-access-policies

For more recent studies, showing even higher levels of support, see Kumiko Vézina (2008, 83 percent willingness) and Graham Stone (2010, 86 percent willingness).

http://eprints.rclis.org/handle/10760/12731
http://eprints.hud.ac.uk/9257

17. See my article "Unanimous faculty votes," *SPARC Open Access Newsletter*, June 2, 2010.
   http://dash.harvard.edu/bitstream/handle/1/4723857/suber_votes
   .htm?sequence=1
After my article appeared, I moved the list of unanimous faculty votes to the Open Access Directory, a wiki, where it has since been enlarged by the community.
   http://oad.simmons.edu/oadwiki/Unanimous_faculty_votes
Note that many but not all the policies adopted by unanimous faculty votes are mandates.

18. This section borrows from several of my previous publications:
"The open access mandate at Harvard," *SPARC Open Access Newsletter*, March 2, 2008.
   http://dash.harvard.edu/bitstream/handle/1/4322574/suber_harvard
   .html?sequence=1
"Three principles for university open access policies," *SPARC Open Access Newsletter*, April 2, 2008.
   http://dash.harvard.edu/bitstream/handle/1/4317659/suber
   _3principles.html?sequence=2
"Open access policy options for funding agencies and universities," *SPARC Open Access Newsletter*, February 2, 2009.
   http://dash.harvard.edu/bitstream/handle/1/4322589/suber
   _oaoptions.html?sequence=1
"Open access in 2010," *SPARC Open Access Newsletter*, January 2, 2011.
   http://dash.harvard.edu/bitstream/handle/1/4736588/suber_oa2010
   .htm?sequence=1

19. This is why strong OA policies at large institutions are so important. The NIH is the largest funder of nonclassified research in the world. Publishers cannot afford to refuse to publish NIH-funded authors, and as a result publisher accommodation of the NIH's OA mandate is 100 percent.
   http://oad.simmons.edu/oadwiki/Publisher_policies_on_NIH-funded
   _authors

20. UK PubMed Central (UKPMC) reported that the percentage of annual deposits that are libre OA, and not merely gratis OA, rose from 7 percent in 2001 to 33 percent in 2009.

http://ukpmc.blogspot.com/2011/04/increasing-amount-of-content
-in-ukpmc.html

In 2010 alone, seven green OA mandates required some degree of libre OA: those from the Library Faculty at Arizona State University, Australian National University, Harvard Business School, Harvard Divinity School, University of Sassari, Sweden's Royal Library, and the Washington State Board for Community and Technical Colleges (SBCTC) on behalf of thirty-four institutions. Whether we consider these to be seven policies (the number of enactments) or forty (the number of institutions covered), the number significantly surpasses the three libre green policies adopted in 2009.

http://dash.harvard.edu/bitstream/handle/1/4725027/suber
_octmandates.htm?sequence=1

Going back farther, since 2007 the Wellcome Trust and UKPMC Funders Group have required green libre OA whenever they pay for publication and not just for the underlying research.

http://www.wellcome.ac.uk/about-us/policy/spotlight-issues
/Open-access/Guides/wtx041316.htm

In 2009, the U.S. Institute of Medicine (IOM) convened a group of major public and private funding agencies, which called on funders of medical research to mandate green libre OA. The group includes the Gates Foundation, Burroughs Wellcome Fund, Merck Company Foundation, Rockefeller Foundation, U.S. Department of Health and Human Services, U.S. Department of Homeland Security, and U.S. Department of State.

http://www.earlham.edu/~peters/fos/2009/05/us-commitment-to
-global-health-should.html

In October 2010, a $20 million funding program from the Gates Foundation, the Next Generation Learning Challenges, mandated libre OA for the results of funded projects.

http://creativecommons.org/weblog/entry/23831

In January 2011, the U.S. Department of Labor and Department of Education announced the Trade Adjustment Assistance Community College and Career Training (TAACCCT), a four-year, $2 billion funding program for open educational resources (OER) mandating libre OA under CC-BY licenses.

http://www.whitehouse.gov/blog/2011/01/20/new-job-training-and
-education-grants-program-launched
http://dash.harvard.edu/bitstream/handle/1/4736319/suber_another
fed.htm?sequence=1

Libre green policies were recommended in the Berkman Center's Evaluation of Private Foundation Copyright Licensing Policies, Practices and Opportunities (August 2009) and in the Ghent Declaration (February 2011).

> http://cyber.law.harvard.edu/sites/cyber.law.harvard.edu/files/OCL
> _for_Foundations_REPORT.pdf
> http://www.openaire.eu/index.php?option=com_content&view=article
> &id=223:seizing-the-opportunity-for-open-access-to-european
> -research-ghent-declaration-published&catid=76:highlights&lang=en

Chapter 5

1. This section borrows from two of my previous publications:
"Open Access Overview"

> http://dash.harvard.edu/bitstream/handle/1/4729737/suber_oaover
> view.htm?sequence=1

"A field guide to misunderstandings about open access," *SPARC Open Access Newsletter*, April 2, 2009.

> http://dash.harvard.edu/bitstream/handle/1/4322571/suber_field
> guide.html?sequence=1

2. For some purposes we must distinguish two kinds of postprint: those that have been peer-reviewed but not copyedited and those that have been both peer-reviewed and copyedited. Some publishers allow authors to deposit the first kind but not the second in an OA repository.

3. This section borrows from my:
"Open access to electronic theses and dissertations (ETDs)," *SPARC Open Access Newsletter*, July 2, 2006.

> http://dash.harvard.edu/bitstream/handle/1/4727443/suber_theses
> .htm?sequence=1

4. See Gail McMillan, "Do ETDs Deter Publishers? Does Web availability count as prior publication? A report on the 4th International Conference on Electronic Theses and Dissertations," *College and Research Libraries News* 62 (6) (June 2001). "[T]he ready availability of ETDs on the Internet does not deter the vast majority of publishers from publishing articles derived from graduate research already available on the Internet."

> http://scholar.lib.vt.edu/staff/gailmac/publications/pubrsETD2001
> .html

The case is less certain for books. See Jennifer Howard, "The Road from Dissertation to Book Has a New Pothole: The Internet," *Chronicle of Higher Education*, April 3, 2011, and the discussion it triggered on the LibLicense list.

> http://chronicle.com/article/The-Road-From-Dissertation-to/126977
> http://www.library.yale.edu/~llicense/ListArchives/1104/msg00028
> .html

5. This section borrows from several of my previous publications:
"Promoting Open Access in the Humanities," *Syllecta Classica*, 16 (2005) 231–246.

> http://dash.harvard.edu/bitstream/handle/1/4729720/suber_promot
> ing.htm?sequence=1

My answers to Richard Poynder's interview questions in "The Basement Interviews: Peter Suber," October 19, 2007.

> http://poynder.blogspot.com/2007/10/basement-interviews-peter
> - suber.html

"Predictions for 2009," *SPARC Open ACcess Newsletter*, December 2, 2008.

> http://www.earlham.edu/~peters/fos/newsletter/12-02-08
> .htm#predictions

6. See the Open Access Directory list of publishers of OA books.

> http://oad.simmons.edu/oadwiki/Publishers_of_OA_books

7. For a review of this and other business models for OA books, see Janneke Adema, "Overview of Open Access Models for eBooks in the Humanities and Social Sciences," Open Access Publishing in European Networks (OAPEN), March 2010.

> http://project.oapen.org/images/documents/openaccessmodels.pdf

Also see the Open Access Directory list of OA book business models.

> http://oad.simmons.edu/oadwiki/OA_book_business_models

8. For some of the most careful empirical studies, see:
John Hilton III, "'Freely ye have received, freely give' (Matthew 10:8): how giving away religious digital books influences the print sales of those books," Master's thesis at Brigham Young University, 2010.

> http://search.lib.byu.edu/byu/id:byu_unicorn4414980

John Hilton III, "Hard Numbers on Free Random House Books," Wide Open, May 6, 2009.

> http://web.archive.org/web/20090510052632/http://www
> .johnhiltoniii.org/hard-numbers-on-free-random-house-books

John Hilton III and David Wiley, "Free: Why Authors Are Giving Books Away on the Internet," *Tech Trends* 54 (2), 2010.

http://hdl.lib.byu.edu/1877/2154

John Hilton III and David Wiley, "The Short-Term Influence of Free Digital Versions of Books on Print Sales," *Journal of Electronic Publishing* 13 (1), Winter 2010.

http://dx.doi.org/10.3998/3336451.0013.101

Brian O'Leary, "The impact of piracy," *Magellan Media*, June 8, 2009.

http://www.magellanmediapartners.com/index.php/mmcp/article/the_impact_of_piracy/

Oriental Institute Publications Office, "The Electronic Publications Initiative of the Oriental Institute of the University of Chicago," The Oriental Institute of the University of Chicago, April 6, 2009.

http://oi.uchicago.edu/research/pubs/epi.html

Springer Science+Business Media, "More than 29,000 titles now live in Google Book Search," press release, March 1, 2007.

http://www.springer.com/librarians/e-content?SG
WID=0-113-6-442110-0

Tim O'Reilly, "Free Downloads vs. Sales: A Publishing Case Study," O'Reilly Radar, June 1, 2007.

http://radar.oreilly.com/archives/2007/06/free-downloads.html

"OAPEN-UK," an ongoing experiment from JISC, October 22, 2010.

http://www.jisc-collections.ac.uk/News/OAPENUKITT

Caren Milloy, "JISC national e-books observatory project: 2007–2010," Joint Information Systems Committee, 2010.

http://www.jiscebooksproject.org/archives/211

For a more comprehensive collection of studies and observations, see the "oa.books.sales" tag library from the Open Access Tracking Project.

http://www.connotea.org/tag/oa.books.sales

9. National Academies Press.

http://www.nap.edu

See Jensen's articles from 2001, 2005, and 2007.

http://chronicle.com/article/Academic-Press-Gives-Away-Its/27430
http://chronicle.com/article/Presses-Have-Little-to-Fear/25775
http://dx.doi.org/10.3998/3336451.0010.206

10. See the AAUP "Statement on Open Access," February 7, 2007.

http://www.aaupnet.org/images/stories/documents/oastatement.pdf
http://www.earlham.edu/~peters/fos/2007/02/aaup-statement-on-open-access.html

Also see its May 2011 Digital Book Publishing Survey.

http://www.aaupnet.org/news-a-publications/news/421-aaup-digital
-book-publishing-survey-report-released

11. This section borrows from several of my previous publications:

"Abridgment as added value," *SPARC Open Access Newsletter*, November 2, 2009.
http://dash.harvard.edu/bitstream/handle/1/4317664/suber
_abridgment.html?sequence=1

"Promoting Open Access in the Humanities," *Syllecta Classica*, 16 (2005) 231–246.
http://dash.harvard.edu/bitstream/handle/1/4729720/suber
_promoting.htm?sequence=1

"Discovery, rediscovery, and open access. Part 1," *SPARC Open Access Newsletter*, August 2, 2010.
http://dash.harvard.edu/bitstream/handle/1/4455489/suber
_discovery.htm?sequence=1

12. For more along these lines, see my article "Open access and the self-correction of knowledge," *SPARC Open Access Newsletter*, June 2, 2008.
http://dash.harvard.edu/bitstream/handle/1/4391168/suber
_selfcorrect.html?sequence=1

13. Ten months before a massive earthquake killed 70,000 people in China's Sichuan Province (on May 12, 2008), an international team of scientists published a prediction of the quake with what *National Geographic* called "eerie" precision. However, *National Geographic* also notes that "there is little reason to believe Chinese officials were aware of the July 2007 study." One of the prediction coauthors, Michael Ellis of the Center for Earthquake Research and Information at the University of Memphis, noted that the "information was effectively locked in an academic journal."
http://news.nationalgeographic.com/news/2008/05/080516
-earthquake-predicted.html

14. This section borrows from several of my previous publications:

"The taxpayer argument for open access," *SPARC Open Access Newsletter*, September 4, 2003.
http://dash.harvard.edu/bitstream/handle/1/4725013/suber_taxpayer
.htm?sequence=1

"Follow-up on the Federal Research Public Access Act," *SPARC Open Access Newsletter*, June 2, 2006.

http://dash.harvard.edu/bitstream/handle/1/3942944/suber_news98
.html?sequence=2#frpaa

My answers to Richard Poynder's interview questions in "The Basement Interviews: Peter Suber," October 19, 2007.

http://poynder.blogspot.com/2007/10/basement-interviews-peter
-suber.html

"A field guide to misunderstandings about open access," *SPARC Open Access Newsletter*, April 2, 2009. See especially section 23.

http://dash.harvard.edu/bitstream/handle/1/4322571/suber_field
guide.html?sequence=1

15. See my article "Knowledge as a public good," *SPARC Open Access Newsletter*, November 2, 2009.

http://dash.harvard.edu/bitstream/handle/1/4391171/suber
_public%20good.html?sequence=1

16. When John Jarvis was the Managing Director of Wiley Europe, he testified before the UK Parliament's House of Commons Select Committee on Science and Technology in March 2004. From his response to Question 19: "[T]here is some evidence that some of the support for open access is coming from outside the research community. . . . Without being pejorative or elitist, I think that is an issue that we should think about very, very carefully, because there are very few members of the public, and very few people in this room, who would want to read some of this scientific information, and in fact draw wrong conclusions from it. . . . I will say again; let us be careful because this rather enticing statement that everybody should be able to see everything could lead to chaos. Speak to people in the medical profession, and they will say the last thing they want are people who may have illnesses reading this information, marching into surgeries and asking things."

http://www.publications.parliament.uk/pa/cm200304/cmselect
/cmsctech/uc399-i/uc39902.htm

Larry Reynolds, editor in chief of the *Journal of Animal Science* argued in a March 2007 editorial that "because the public has no idea how to read, interpret, or put published science into context, immediate public access will lead to sensationalized use, or misuse, of science."

http://www.asas.org/bulletin_article.asp?a=9&s=&r=3

In a May 2007 blog post, physician R. W. Donnell accused the *New England Journal of Medicine* of "tabloid based medicine" for providing OA to an editorial and peer-reviewed article on the drug Avandia. The problem seems to be that the two OA pieces triggered "millions of Google search queries for Avandia."

> http://doctorrw.blogspot.com/2007/05/tabloid-based-medicine
> -trumps-evidence.html

17. See Richard K. Johnson, "Will Research Sharing Keep Pace with the Internet?" *The Journal of Neuroscience* 26 (37) (September 13, 2006), pp. 9349–9351. "The large audience for freely accessible scientific knowledge may be surprising to many, but the hunger for it is apparent from experience of the National Library of Medicine (NLM). A few years ago, NLM transformed its fee-based index and abstracts of biomedical journal articles to free availability on the Web as PubMed. Use of the database increased 100-fold once it became freely available. The potential scope of this usage could never have been anticipated by looking solely at use of the controlled-access version. Who are these new readers? They surely include scientists around the globe at institutions that may not be able to afford needed journals. They also may be researchers in unexpected fields, search engine users who didn't realize previously they could use work in a seemingly unrelated field. They may be students, patients or their families, physicians, community health workers, or others from the general public: taxpayers who finance so much biomedical research."

> http://www.jneurosci.org/content/26/37/9349.full

As early as 2004, Donald Lindberg, then-director of the National Library of Medicine, reported that the NLM's OA web site had more than one million visitors per day and "close to a billion a year. . . . A good, heavy part of that are consumers." Quoted in Gene Koprowski, "The Web: Patients heal themselves online," United Press International, August 14, 2004.

> http://www.upi.com/Science_News/2004/08/04/The-Web-Patients
> -heal-themselves-online/UPI-96731091633186

18. For a good list of nonprofit disease advocacy organizations supporting OA for publicly-funded research in the United States, see the membership list of the Alliance for Taxpayer Access.

> http://www.taxpayeraccess.org/membership/index.shtml

19. "Large Majorities of U.S. Adults Support Easy—and Free—Online Access to Federally-Funded Research Findings on Health Issues and Other Topics," *Harris Interactive*, May 31, 2006.

> http://www.harrisinteractive.com/vault/Harris-Interactive-Poll
> -Research-ATA-Statement-of-Support-2006-05.pdf

20. If you believe that lay readers don't care to read peer-reviewed medical research and couldn't understand it if they tried, and if you only have time to read one eye-opening testimonial, read Sharon Terry's.

http://crln.acrl.org/content/66/7/522.full.pdf

21. For more on the possibility of providing OA to some, such as the citizens of one country, and denying it to others, see my article "The taxpayer argument for open access," *SPARC Open Access Newsletter*, September 4, 2003.

> http://dash.harvard.edu/bitstream/handle/1/4725013/suber_taxpayer .htm?sequence=1

22. This section borrows from several of my previous publications:
"Thoughts on first and second-order scholarly judgments," *SPARC Open Access Newsletter*, April 8, 2002.

> http://dash.harvard.edu/bitstream/handle/1/4727447/suber _thoughts.htm?sequence=1

My answers to James Morrison's interview questions in *The Technology Source*, September/October 2002.

> http://www.technologysource.org/article/free_online_scholarship _movement

My answers to Cy Dillon's interview questions in *Virginia Libraries* 54 (2) (April/May/June 2008), pp. 7–12.

> http://dash.harvard.edu/bitstream/handle/1/4724180/suber_dillonin terview.htm?sequence=1

23. On the claim that information overload didn't start with the internet, see Ann Blair, *Too Much to Know: Managing Scholarly Information Before the Modern Age*, Yale University Press, November 2010.

> http://yalepress.yale.edu/yupbooks/book.asp?isbn=9780300112511

On the claim that the size of the internet and the power of search are both growing quickly, see "Can search tame the wild web? Can open access help?" *SPARC Open Access Newsletter*, December 2, 2005.

> http://dash.harvard.edu/bitstream/handle/1/4727442/suber_wildweb .htm?sequence=1

24. Clay Shirky, "It's Not Information Overload. It's Filter Failure," Web 2.0 Expo NY, September 16–19, 2008.

> http://web2expo.blip.tv/file/1277460

25. Also see Clifford Lynch, "Open Computation: Beyond Human-Reader-Centric Views of Scholarly Literatures," *Open Access: Key Strategic, Technical and Economic Aspects*, Neil Jacobs (ed.), Chandos Publishing, 2006, pp. 185–193.
"Traditional open access is, in my view, a probable (but not certain) prerequisite

for the emergence of fully developed large-scale computational approaches to the scholarly literature."

    http://www.cni.org/staff/cliffpubs/OpenComputation.htm

Chapter 6

1. This section borrows from several of my previous publications:
"Open Access Overview."

    http://dash.harvard.edu/bitstream/handle/1/4729737/suber_oaover
    view.htm?sequence=1

"The mandates of January," *SPARC Open Access Newsletter*, February 2, 2008.
    http://dash.harvard.edu/bitstream/handle/1/4322581/suber_january
    .html?sequence=1

"A bill to overturn the NIH policy," *SPARC Open Access Newsletter*, October 2, 2008.

    http://dash.harvard.edu/bitstream/handle/1/4322592/suber_nihbill
    .html?sequence=1

"A field guide to misunderstandings about open access," *SPARC Open Access Newsletter*, April 2, 2009.

    http://dash.harvard.edu/bitstream/handle/1/4322571/suber_field
    guide.html?sequence=1

2. See the OAD list of publisher policies on NIH-funded authors.
    http://oad.simmons.edu/oadwiki/Publisher_policies_on_NIH-funded
    _authors

3. The bill was the so-called Fair Copyright in Research Works Act, introduced by Rep. John Conyers (D-MI) in September 2008 and again in the next session of Congress in February 2009. In both cases it died without a vote. See my articles on each introduction of the bill:

"A bill to overturn the NIH policy," *SPARC Open Access Newsletter*, October 2, 2008.

    http://dash.harvard.edu/bitstream/handle/1/4322592/suber_nihbill
    .html?sequence=1

"Re-introduction of the bill to kill the NIH policy," *SPARC Open Access Newsletter*, March 2, 2009.

    http://dash.harvard.edu/bitstream/handle/1/4391154/suber_reintro
    .html?sequence=1

4. However, as we've seen (in section 3.3 on gratis/libre) most OA journals still settle for gratis OA even though they could just as easily obtain the rights for libre OA.

5. See L. Ray Patterson, "A Response to Mr. Y'Barbo's Reply," *Journal of Intellectual Property Law* 5 (1997).

Chapter 7

1. This section borrows from several of my previous publications:

"No-fee open-access journals," *SPARC Open Access Newsletter*, November 2, 2006.
> http://dash.harvard.edu/bitstream/handle/1/4552050/suber_nofee
> .htm?sequence=1

"Good facts, bad predictions," *SPARC Open Access Newsletter*, June 2, 2006.
> http://dash.harvard.edu/bitstream/handle/1/4391309/suber_facts
> .htm?sequence=1

"Will open access undermine peer review?" *SPARC Open Access Newsletter*, September 2, 2007.
> http://dash.harvard.edu/bitstream/handle/1/4322578/suber_peer
> .html?sequence=1

"Ten challenges for open-access journals," *SPARC Open Access Newsletter*, October 2, 2009.
> http://dash.harvard.edu/bitstream/handle/1/4316131/suber
> _10challenges.html?sequence=2

2. See John Houghton and Peter Sheehan, "The Economic Impact of Enhanced Access to Research Findings," Centre for Strategic Economic Studies, Victoria University Working Paper No. 23, July 2006.
> http://www.cfses.com/documents/wp23.pdf

John Houghton, Colin Steele, and Peter Sheehan, "Research Communication Costs in Australia: Emerging Opportunities and Benefits," Australia's Department of Education, Science and Training, September 2006.
> http://www.dest.gov.au/NR/rdonlyres/0ACB271F-EA7D-4FAF-B3F7
> -0381F441B175/13935/DEST_Research_Communications_Cost
> _Report_Sept2006.pdf

Also see Alma Swan's February 2010 study, based on Houghton's model, of the costs and benefits of OA policies at universities.
> http://www.jisc.ac.uk/publications/programmerelated/2010
> /howtoopenaccess.aspx

Also see Stevan Harnad's March 2010 article building on Houghton's finding that the economic benefits of green OA exceed the costs more than fortyfold.

http://eprints.ecs.soton.ac.uk/18514

For Houghton's other studies on the economic impact of OA policies, see the home page for his research project on the Economic Implications of Alternative Scholarly Publishing Models (EI-ASPM).

http://www.cfses.com/EI-ASPM

For the publisher critique of Houghton's research, see the two joint statements by the Publishers Association (PA), the Association of Learned and Professional Society Publishers (ALPSP), and the International Association of Scientific, Technical and Medical Publishers (STM), both dated February 2009.

http://www.publishers.org.uk/images/stories/AboutPA/Newsletters
/pa-alpsp-stm_joint_statement.pdf
http://www.fep-fee.be/documents/TAcommentsonH-OJISCreport
-final.doc

Also see the STM press release, with links to related documents, "STM challenges JISC over validity of latest open access advocacy," April 2010.

http://web.archive.org/web/20100424033638/http://www.stm-assoc
.org/news.php?id=294&PHPSESSID=08b2a9f56c8b6e7fec0eeac997bd
c0b3

For the major replies to the publisher critiques, see the replies from JISC (undated but c. April 2009) and Houghton himself (January 2010).

http://www.jisc.ac.uk/media/documents/publications/responseone
iaspmreport.pdf
http://www.cfses.com/EI-ASPM/Comments-on-Hall(Houghton&
Oppenheim).pdf

3. See "Heading for the Open Road: Costs and Benefits of Transitions in Scholarly Communications," Research Information Network, April 7, 2011.

http://www.rin.ac.uk/our-work/communicating-and-disseminating
-research/heading-open-road-costs-and-benefits-transitions-s

4. Charles W. Bailey Jr., Karen Coombs, Jill Emery, Anne Mitchell, Chris Morris, Spencer Simons, and Robert Wright, "Institutional Repositories," ARL SPEC Kit 292, July, 2006. "Implementers [of repositories at ARL libraries] report a range of start-up costs from $8,000 to $1,800,000, with a mean of $182,550 and a median of $45,000. . . . The range for ongoing operations budgets for implementers is $8,600 to $500,000, with a mean of $113,543 and median of $41,750."

http://www.arl.org/bm~doc/spec292web.pdf

An informal 2005 survey by Rebecca Kemp found that the costs of setting up a repository ranged from \$5,770 (CILEA) to \$1,706,765 (Cambridge University) and that yearly maintenance ranged from \$36,000 (National University of Ireland) to \$285,000 (MIT).

> http://www.earlham.edu/~peters/fos/2005/11/costs-of-oa-repositories.html

In 2001, Caltech reported that its set-up costs were less than \$1,000.

> http://web.archive.org/web/20041014190643/http://www.arl.org/sparc/pubs/enews/aug01.html#6

5. For more on the "some pay for all" business models, see "Four analogies to clean energy," *SPARC Open Access Newsletter*, February 2, 2010.

> http://dash.harvard.edu/bitstream/handle/1/4315928/suber_4analogies.html?sequence=2

6. For details on the variety of business models for OA journals, see the Open Access Directory list of OA journal business models.

> http://oad.simmons.edu/oadwiki/OA_journal_business_models

Also see Raym Crow, "Income Models for Supporting Open Access," SPARC, October 2009.

> http://www.arl.org/sparc/publisher/incomemodels

7. Suenje Dallmeier-Tiessen et al., "Highlights from the SOAP (Study of Open Access Publishing) project survey. What Scientists Think about Open Access Publishing," arXiv, January 28, 2011. "In total 89% of published researchers answering to the survey thought that journals publishing open access articles were beneficial for their field. When analysed by discipline, this fraction was higher than 90% in most of the humanities and social sciences, and oscillating around 80% for Chemistry, Astronomy, Physics, Engineering and related disciplines."

> http://arxiv.org/abs/1101.5260

8. On the percentage of OA journals charging author-side fees, see Stuart Shieber, "What percentage of open-access journals charge publication fees?" *The Occasional Pamphlet*, May 29, 2009.

> http://blogs.law.harvard.edu/pamphlet/2009/05/29/what-percentage-of-open-access-journals-charge-publication-fees

On the percentage of TA journals charging author-side fees, see Cara Kaufman and Alma Wills, "The Facts about Open Access," Association of Learned and Professional Society Publishers, 2005.

> http://www.alpsp.org/ngen_public/article.asp?id=200&did=47&aid=270&st=&oaid=-1

On the percentage of authors paying fees out of pocket at fee-based OA journals, see Suenje Dallmeier-Tiessen et al., "Highlights from the SOAP project survey. What Scientists Think about Open Access Publishing," a preprint on deposit in arXiv, January 28, 2011, p. 9, table 4.

> http://arxiv.org/abs/1101.5260

Also see my two articles on no-fee OA journals:

"Good facts, bad predictions," *SPARC Open Access Newsletter*, June 2, 2006.
> http://dash.harvard.edu/bitstream/handle/1/4391309/suber_facts
> .htm?sequence=1

"No-fee open-access journals," *SPARC Open Access Newsletter*, November 2, 2006.
> http://dash.harvard.edu/bitstream/handle/1/4552050/suber_nofee
> .htm?sequence=1

9. See Anuar Bin Shafiei, "An exploratory study into an intermediary service organisation handling author fees on behalf of academic libraries," *Pleiade Management & Consultancy*, October 15, 2010. See section 4.4. 100 percent of responding members of the Open Access Scholarly Publishers Association (OASPA) who published fee-based OA journals, surveyed in July-August 2010, offered some kind of fee waivers. 91 percent prevented editors from knowing about fee-waiver requests during peer review.

> http://www.pleiade.nl/Serviceorganisationauthorfees.pdf
> http://www.oaspa.org/docs/oa_fee_study.pdf

10. For a more detailed response to these calculations, see "Good facts, bad predictions," *SPARC Open Access Newsletter*, June 2, 2006.

> http://dash.harvard.edu/bitstream/handle/1/4391309/suber_facts
> .htm?sequence=1

Today, not only do 70 percent of OA journals charge no author-side fees (see Shieber in note 8), but 59 percent of fees paid at fee-based journals are paid by funding agencies and only 24 percent by universities (see Suenje Dallmeier-Tiessen et al. in note 7).

11. Many of the funds set up by universities to pay publication fees on behalf of faculty refuse to pay fees at double-dipping hybrid journals. For example, the fund at the University of Calgary will only pay fees at hybrid journals "that reduce subscription fees in response to the take-up of their Open Access programs. . . ."

> http://library.ucalgary.ca/services/for-faculty/open-access-authors
> -fund/open-access-authors-fund-frequently-asked-questions-faq#4

Funds at many other institutions will not pay fees at any hybrid journals. For example, see Harvard's HOPE (Harvard Open-Access Publishing Equity) fund.

http://osc.hul.harvard.edu/hope

12. On the AAP/PSP figures, see John Tagler, "From the Executive Director's Desk," *Professional Scholarly Publishing Bulletin*, Spring 2011. Tagler notes that "the two largest open access publishers did not submit data on their publishing programs so the analysis covers open access patterns across a universe where paid circulation, rather than [an OA business model], is the principal source of revenue."

http://www.pspcentral.org/documents/PSPWinter-Spring2011.pdf

See the SHERPA list of hybrid journal publishers. When I checked it April 29, 2011, it listed 91 journal publishers, including all of the largest.

http://www.sherpa.ac.uk/romeo/PaidOA.html

"Report from the SOAP (Study of Open Access Publishing) Symposium," January 2011.

http://project-soap.eu/report-from-the-soap-symposium

13. See "Open access in 2006," *SPARC Open Access Newsletter*, January 2, 2007.
http://dash.harvard.edu/bitstream/handle/1/4729246/suber_oa2006
.htm?sequence=1

The hybrid OA landscape hasn't changed much since January 2007, when I summarized the situation this way:

Some hybrid programs are good-faith, even optimistic experiments; some look grudging or cynical. Some charge low fees and let participating authors retain copyright; some charge high fees and still demand the copyright. Some provide OA to the full published edition, some only to an enfeebled truncation stripped of active links. Some reduce subscription prices in proportion to author uptake; some use a frank "double charge" business model. Some let authors deposit articles in repositories independent of the publisher; some allow free online access only from sites they control. Some don't try to meddle with author funding contracts; some charge authors who want to comply with prior funding obligations. Some continue to allow immediate self-archiving for non-participating authors; some impose embargoes or fees on self-archiving. The positive spin on this wide range of policies is that publishers are fully exploring the hybrid journal space for variations that satisfy their constraints. I do think that's good even if I also think some current models are cynical or useless. To make the same point without the spin, some want to encourage author uptake and some don't seem to care as long as they have subscriptions.

Also see "Predictions for 2006," *SPARC Open Access Newsletter*, December 2, 2006. "The big question for [hybrid OA] publishers is whether they want author uptake badly enough to make it attractive. Will the existence of subscription revenue as a safety net kill the incentives to make the OA option succeed?"

http://dash.harvard.edu/bitstream/handle/1/4391164/suber
_2006predict.htm?sequence=1

Also see "Nine questions for hybrid journal programs," *SPARC Open Access Newsletter*, September 2, 2006.

http://dash.harvard.edu/bitstream/handle/1/4552044/suber_hybrid
questions.htm?sequence=1

14. BioMed Central was acquired by Springer in 2008 and remains OA and profitable. It also has a membership program.

http://www.biomedcentral.com

The Public Library of Science publishes seven journals; some make surpluses and some don't. From a financial standpoint, PLoS ONE is most successful and has inspired imitations from a handful of predominantly TA publishers.

http://www.plos.org

See PLoS ONE and my article on its imitators.

http://www.plosone.org

"Recent watershed events," *SPARC Open Access Newsletter*, March 2, 2011.

http://dash.harvard.edu/bitstream/handle/1/4736559/suber_water
shed.htm?sequence=1

MedKnow not only makes revenue from print editions but also from advertising, association memberships, and author reprints.

http://www.medknow.com

Another nonprofit OA journal making a surplus is *Optics Express* from the Optical Society of America. It routinely has one of the highest impact factors in its field and in 2006 was the most cited journal in optics.

http://www.opticsexpress.org
http://www.photonicsonline.com/article.mvc/IOptics-ExpressI-IOp
tics-LettersI-Top-Rated-J-0001

15. On how open-source journal management software, and OJS in particular, reduces publication costs, see Brian D. Edgar and John Willinsky, "A Survey of Scholarly Journals Using Open Journal Systems," *Scholarly and Research Communication*, 1, 2 (April 2010). See especially table 14.

http://journals.sfu.ca/src/index.php/src/article/view/24/41

"Over 9000 OJS Installations," Public Knowledge Project, April 6, 2011.
http://pkp.sfu.ca/node/3695

See the OAD list of Free and open-source journal management software.
http://oad.simmons.edu/oadwiki/Free_and_open-source_journal
_management_software

16. John Houghton's research from January 2009 estimates savings from gold OA, not just from green OA. "For UK higher education, these journal article cost differences would have amounted to savings of around £80 million per annum circa 2007 from a shift from subscription access to open access publishing. . . ."

http://www.jisc.ac.uk/media/documents/publications/summary
-economicoa.pdf

http://www.jisc.ac.uk/publications/reports/2009/economicpublishing
modelsfinalreport.aspx

Also see Julian Fisher, "Scholarly Publishing Re-invented: Real Costs and Real Freedoms in the Journal of Electronic Publishing," *Journal of Electronic Publishing*, Spring 2008. "Deploying newly available tools and approaches to article production in a collaborative manner offer dramatic reductions in cost, up to two orders of magnitude."

http://hdl.handle.net/2027/spo.3336451.0011.204

Also see Brian Edgar and John Willinsky (April 2010), ibid., table 15. Of surveyed OSJ-using journals, 29 percent claimed zero expenses, 20 percent claimed expenses between $1 and $1,000, and 31 percent claimed expenses between $1,001 and $10k. 44 percent operated on zero revenue, 16 percent on revenue between $1 and $1,000, and 24 percent on revenue between $1,001 and $10k.

http://journals.sfu.ca/src/index.php/src/article/view/24/41

17. Jan Velterop, post to the SSP-L discussion list August 6, 2003. Apparently the post is no longer online.

18. A March 2010 study by Donald King showed that if all toll-access journals converted to fee-based OA, and if the average fee was $1,500, then the one-year cost of paying the fees for U.S. authors would be $427.5 million (or 0.76 percent of of the U.S. R&D budget). If the average fee was $2,500, the cost would be $712.5 million (or 1.27% of the US R&D budget). Heather Morrison used King's data to calculate that the conversion could result in $3.4 billion in savings in the United States alone. In a follow-up report, Morrison calculated that the more than $2 billion profit earned by Elsevier and Lexis Nexis in 2009

would pay for a year's worth of all the peer-reviewed journal articles published around world at a per-article fee of $1,383.

> http://www.dlib.org/dlib/march10/king/03king.html
> http://poeticeconomics.blogspot.com/2010/03/us-systemic-savings-from-full-shift-to.html
> http://poeticeconomics.blogspot.com/2010/04/elsevier-2009-2-billion-profits-could.html

19. See the Open Access Directory list of OA journal funds.
> http://oad.simmons.edu/oadwiki/OA_journal_funds

Also see the Compact for Open-Access Publishing Equity (COPE), a commitment to launch a fund and persuade other institutions to follow suit.

> http://www.oacompact.org

20. See the SCOAP3 home page.
> http://www.scoap3.org

Peter Suber, "Eleventh hour for SCOAP3," *SPARC Open Access Newsletter*, December 2, 2010.

> http://dash.harvard.edu/bitstream/handle/1/4736587/suber_scoap3.htm?sequence=1

"SCOAP3 Global Partnership Meets and Decides to Move Forward!" SCOAP3 press release, April 12, 2011.

> http://www.scoap3.org/news/news85.html

21. See "Flipping a journal to open access," *SPARC Open Access Newsletter*, October 2, 2007.

> http://dash.harvard.edu/bitstream/handle/1/4322572/suber_flipping.html?sequence=1

Chapter 8

1. This chapter borrows from two of my previous publications:

"Will open access undermine peer review?" *SPARC Open Access Newsletter*, September 2, 2007.

> http://dash.harvard.edu/bitstream/handle/1/4322578/suber_peer.html?sequence=1

"A bill to overturn the NIH policy," *SPARC Open Access Newsletter*, October 2, 2008.

> http://dash.harvard.edu/bitstream/handle/1/4322592/suber_nihbill.html?sequence=1

2. arXiv.

    http://arxiv.org

American Physical Society (APS).

    http://www.aps.org

Institute of Physics (IOP).

    http://www.iop.org

APS mirror of arXiv (launched December 1999).

    http://aps.arxiv.org

IOP mirror of arXiv (launched September 2006).

    http://eprintweb.org

See Alma Swan's interview with the APS and IOP, in which "both societies said they could not identify any losses of subscriptions" due to OA archiving.

    http://eprints.ecs.soton.ac.uk/11006

3. "NIH research: Widening access, building collaboration," *The Lancet*, October 6, 2004.

    http://dx.doi.org/10.1016/S0140-6736(04)17232-2

4. One hearing was convened by Rep. John Conyers (D-MI) for the House Judiciary Committee Subcommittee on Courts, the Internet, and Intellectual Property (September 11, 2008), and the other by Rep. William Lacy Clay (D-MO) for the House Committee on Government Oversight and Reform Subcommittee on Information Policy, the Census, and National Archives (July 29, 2010).

    Testimony from the 2008 hearing.

    http://judiciary.house.gov/hearings/printers/110th/44326.PDF

Testimony from the 2010 hearing.

    http://republicans.oversight.house.gov/index.php?option=com
    _content&view=article&id=922%3A07-29-2010-information

    -policy-qpublic-access-to-federally-funded-researchq&catid=14&Itemid

At the 2008 hearing, the executive director of the American Physiological Society (APS) was among the publisher-witnesses predicting that the NIH policy would cause cancellations. But the NIH policy allowed a twelve-month embargo, and the APS voluntarily made its own papers OA after a twelve-month embargo. In an interview a year later (October 2009), he conceded the lack of evidence. "We haven't had enough time to see an impact."

    http://www.the-scientist.com/blog/display/56046

In addition to the natural experiments resulting from the funder and university green OA mandates, there is a large-scale study in progress, Publishing and the Ecology of European Research (PEER).

http://www.peerproject.eu

5. Steve Hitchcock, "The effect of open access and downloads ('hits') on citation impact: A bibliography of studies," Open Citation Project, continually updated.

http://opcit.eprints.org/oacitation-biblio.html

6. "NPG position statement on open access publishing and subscription business models," January 6, 2011.

http://www.nature.com/press_releases/statement.html

7. "Letter supporting NIH Proposal," Association of College and Research Libraries, November 16, 2004.

http://www.ala.org/ala/mgrps/divs/acrl/issues/washingtonwatch
/ALA_print_layout_1_168551_168551.cfm

8. Chris Beckett and Simon Inger, "Self-Archiving and Journal Subscriptions: Co-existence or Competition? An International Survey of Librarians' Preferences," *Publishing Research Consortium*, October 26, 2006.

http://www.publishingresearch.net/documents/Self-archiving_report
.pdf

Also see Steve Hitchcock's collection of other objections to the PRC study, with replies from Beckett and Inger.

http://www.eprints.org/community/blog/index.php?/archives/163
-Self-Archiving-and-Journal-Subscriptions-Co-existence-or-Competition
.html

9. "ALPSP survey of librarians on factors in journal cancellation," Association of Learned and Professional Society Publishers, March 30, 2006.

http://www.alpsp.org/ForceDownload.asp?id=53

10. On ASCB, see Jonathan B. Weitzman, "The Society Lady" (an interview with Elizabeth Marincola, then executive director of the ASCB), *Open Access Now*, October 6, 2003.

http://www.biomedcentral.com/openaccess/archive/?page=features&i
ssue=6

On Medknow, see D. K. Sahu and Ramesh C. Parma, "Open Access in India," in Neil Jacobs (ed.) *Open Access: Key strategic, technical, and economic aspects*, Chandos Publishing Ltd, 2006.

http://openmed.nic.in/1599/01/Open_Access_in_India.pdf

11. See the Hindawi Publishing press release, "2009: A Year of Strong Growth for Hindawi," January 6, 2010.

https://mx2.arl.org/lists/sparc-oaforum/Message/5326.html
For the rise of submissions to Hindawi journals, see this series of company press releases from mid-2007 to early 2011.

> https://mx2.arl.org/Lists/SPARC-OAForum/Message/3793.html
> https://mx2.arl.org/Lists/SPARC-OAForum/Message/4829.html
> https://mx2.arl.org/lists/sparc-oaforum/Message/5326.html
> https://mx2.arl.org/Lists/SPARC-OAForum/Message/5581.html
> https://mx2.arl.org/Lists/SPARC-OAForum/Message/5715.html

12. See the Springer press release on the purchase of BMC, October 7, 2008.
> https://mx2.arl.org/Lists/SPARC-OAForum/Message/4605.html

Chapter 9

1. This section borrows from two of my previous publications:
"Reflections on OA/TA coexistence," *SPARC Open Access Newsletter*, March 2, 2005.

> http://dash.harvard.edu/bitstream/handle/1/4391157/suber
> _coexistence.htm?sequence=1

"Trends Favoring Open Access," *CT Watch* 3 (3), Fall 2007.

> http://www.ctwatch.org/quarterly/print.php%3Fp=81.html

2. On the dangers of thinking that if something is not free online, then it's not worth reading, see "The Ellen Roche story" and "Comments on the Ellen Roche Story," both in the *Free Online Scholarship Newsletter*, August 23, 2001.

> http://dash.harvard.edu/bitstream/handle/1/4725003/suber_roche
> .htm?sequence=1
> http://dash.harvard.edu/bitstream/handle/1/4725201/suber
> _rochecomments.htm?sequence=1

3. How can we reconcile unanimous faculty votes for strong OA policies with the evidence that faculty have been slow to pay attention to OA and understand it? See "Unanimous faculty votes," *SPARC Open Access Newsletter*, June 2, 2010.

> Campuses where faculty members vote unanimously for OA policies . . .
> are not random exceptions to this current trend. They are cultivated
> exceptions to this current trend. More, they are gradually reversing the
> trend itself. They are campuses where policy proponents have carefully
> educated their colleagues about the issues and patiently answered
> their questions, objections, and misunderstandings. . . . One lesson: If

your campus is considering an OA policy, be patient. Let the education process take as long as it takes. . . .

http://dash.harvard.edu/bitstream/handle/1/4723857/suber_vote s.htm?sequence=1

Chapter 10

1. The Directory of Open Access Journals.
   http://www.doaj.org

2. See the Open Access Directory list of OA journal funds.
   http://oad.simmons.edu/oadwiki/OA_journal_funds

3. Open Access Scholarly Publishers Association (OASPA). See especially the OASPA membership list and code of conduct.
   http://www.oaspa.org
   http://www.oaspa.org/members.php
   http://www.oaspa.org/conduct.php

4. See the SHERPA RoMEO database.
   http://www.sherpa.ac.uk/romeo

5. See the Open Access Directory list of author addenda.
   http://oad.simmons.edu/oadwiki/Author_addenda

6. See the Registry of Open Access Repositories, the Directory of Open Access Repositories, and the Open Access Directory list of Disciplinary Repositories.
   http://roar.eprints.org
   http://www.opendoar.org
   http://oad.simmons.edu/oadwiki/Disciplinary_repositories

7. See OpenDepot, OpenAire, Academia, and Mendeley.
   http://opendepot.org
   http://www.openaire.eu
   http://www.academia.edu
   http://www.mendeley.com

8. See the Open Access Directory list of data repositories.
   http://oad.simmons.edu/oadwiki/Data_repositories
   Also see the list from DataCite, the British Library, BioMed Central, and the Digital Curation Centre.
   http://datacite.org/repolist

ADDITIONAL RESOURCES

More About OA Itself

Open Access Directory (OAD). A wiki I co-founded with Robin Peek in April 2008.

    http://oad.simmons.edu

Also see these major lists from the OAD (among other OAD lists in separate categories below):

- Events
  http://oad.simmons.edu/oadwiki/Events
- OA by the numbers
  http://oad.simmons.edu/oadwiki/OA_by_the_numbers
- Timeline
  http://oad.simmons.edu/oadwiki/Timeline

Open Access Scholarly Information Sourcebook (OASIS). A compendium of practical steps for implementing OA, from Leslie Chan and Alma Swan.

    http://www.openoasis.org/

Open Access Tracking Project (OATP). A real-time alert service I launched in April 2009.

    http://oad.simmons.edu/oadwiki/OA_tracking_project

More on Green OA (OA through Repositories)

Directory of Open Access Repositories (OpenDoar). With ROAR, one of the two major lists of OA repositories.

    http://www.opendoar.org/

Registry of Open Access Repositories (ROAR). With OpenDoar, one of the two major lists of OA repositories.

    http://roar.eprints.org/

Registry of Open Access Repositories Mandatory Archiving Policies (ROAR-MAP). The best list of green OA policies at funding agencies and universities.

    http://www.eprints.org/openaccess/policysignup/

SHERPA RoMEO. The best database of journal publisher policies on OA archiving.

    http://www.sherpa.ac.uk/romeo/

More on Gold OA (OA through Journals)

Directory of Open Access Journals (DOAJ). The best directory of quality-controlled OA journals.

http://www.doaj.org/

OA journal business models. A list from the Open Access Directory.

http://oad.simmons.edu/oadwiki/OA_journal_business_models

Open Access Scholarly Publishers Association (OASPA). The professional association of OA publishers.

http://www.oaspa.org/

More on OA Advocacy

Advocacy organizations for OA. A list from the Open Access Directory.

http://oad.simmons.edu/oadwiki/Advocacy_organizations_for_OA

Scholarly Publishing and Academic Resources Coalition (SPARC). A major OA advocacy organization in the US.

http://www.arl.org/sparc/

Also see the SPARC spinoff, the Alliance for Taxpayer Access (ATA). A major voice for OA in Congress.

http://www.taxpayeraccess.org/

Enabling Open Scholarship (EOS). A major advocacy organization for university OA policies.

http://www.openscholarship.org/

More of My Own Work on OA

Harvard Open Access Project (HOAP). My current home and major affiliation since July 2011.

http://cyber.law.harvard.edu/hoap

Open Access Overview. My brief introduction to OA, in English and several other languages.

http://www.earlham.edu/~peters/fos/overview.htm

Very Brief Introduction to Open Access. My briefer introduction, in English and many other languages.

http://www.earlham.edu/~peters/fos/brief.htm

Open Access News (OAN). My blog on OA from May 2002 to April 2010. It remains online with a searchable archive.

    http://www.earlham.edu/~peters/fos/fosblog.html

I currently blog at Google+, mostly on OA.

    http://www.google.com/profiles/peter.suber

SPARC Open Access Newsletter (SOAN). My newsletter on OA, since March 2001.

    http://www.earlham.edu/~peters/fos/newsletter/archive.htm

Writings on Open Access. A bibliography of my major pieces on OA.

    http://www.earlham.edu/~peters/fos/oawritings.htm

Additional Reading

Bailey, Jr., Charles W. 2010. *Transforming Scholarly Publishing through Open Access: A Bibliography*. Digital Scholarship. Available in OA and print editions.

    http://www.digital-scholarship.org/tsp/w/tsp.html

Also see the *Bibliography of open access*, a wiki-based descendant of the 2005 edition of Bailey's bibliography, hosted at the Open Access Directory and created with Bailey's generous permission.

    http://oad.simmons.edu/oadwiki/Bibliography_of_open_access

Please also see Peter Suber's online page of updates and supplements to this book.

    http://bit.ly/oa-book.

INDEX

Business models. *See* Artificial scarcity; Funding; Open-access journals and publishers; Revenue; Subsidies; Toll-access (or conventional) journals and publishers

California Institute of Technology (Caltech), 208–209n4
Cambridge University, 208–209n4
Cancer Research UK, 195n9
Career-building for faculty, 12–13, 15, 16, 60, 130. *See also* Attribution; Authors; Impact; Prestige; Promotion and tenure
Carnegie Mellon University, 192n3
Censorship, 26
Center for Earthquake Research and Information, 202n13
Centre for Research Communications, 195n9
Chan, Leslie, 219
Charities, 14, 83–85, 160
Citations. *See* Attribution; Impact
Clark, Len, xii
Clarke, Roger, 185n16
Clay, William Lacy, 215n4
College of Mount Saint Vincent, 193n5
Compact for Open-Access Publishing Equity (COPE), 214n19
Concordia University, 194n5
Congress, 72, 152
Conseil Européen pour la Recherche Nucléaire (CERN), 146–147. *See also* Sponsoring Consortium for Open Access Publishing in Particle Physics SCOAP3

Consorzio Interuniversitario Lombardo per l'Elaborazione Automatica (CILEA), 208–209n4
Contracts, 23, 33, 68, 83–88, 129, 172, 196n15
Conventional journals and publishers. *See* Toll-access (or conventional) journals and publishers
Conyers, John, 206n3, 215n4
Coombs, Karen, 208n4
Copyright, 5, 129–132. *See also* Access; Attribution; Fair use; Libre OA; Licenses; Mandates; Misunderstandings; Permission; Policies; Public domain; Waivers
abolition of, 21
all-rights-reserved, 67–70, 72–73
author control of, 9, 77–78
Budapest/Bethesda/Berlin (BBB) statements and, 7–8, 19, 71
copyright holder consent, 9, 21, 22, 68, 125
derivative works, 8, 69, 74
expiration of, 69
as incentive for author productivity, 129–132
limited role for, 7–8
protects publishers more than authors, 5, 130
protects revenue, 125, 126, 130
publishers and, 5, 9, 34, 39, 58–60, 125–132, 156
reform of, 21, 44, 132, 166
rights retention and, 80–83, 87, 90, 93, 126–129, 149
as temporary government-granted monopoly, 39
toll-access journals and, 125–126, 129

Hybrid journals, 140–142, 210–211n11, 211–212n13. *See also* Journals (in general); Open-access journals and publishers; Toll-access (or conventional) journals and publishers

Impact. *See also* Attribution; Authors; Career-building for faculty; Citations; Prestige
  citation impact, 15–16, 50, 102, 145, 154, 178–179n6, 187n2, 216n5
  writing for impact rather than money, 2, 10, 38, 130
Incentives, 2, 15–17, 19, 57, 60, 86, 111, 121–122, 129–131, 139, 155–157. *See also* Authors; Career-building for faculty; Impact; Libraries; Mandates; Open-access journals and publishers; Policies; Prestige; Researchers; Revenue; Toll-access (or conventional) journals and publishers
  for authors to make their work OA, 15–17, 29–48, 57, 60, 78, 86, 87, 88, 121–122
  for authors to publish in certain journals, 60
  for authors to write, 2, 12–13, 15, 19, 129–131
  for developers to create tools optimized for OA literature, 121–122
  for editors and referees to participate in peer review, 19
  for funding agencies and universities to adopt OA policies, 14, 77–78
  for libraries to cancel toll-access journals, 30–32, 157–159
  for libraries to subscribe to toll-access journals, 155–157
  for publishers to lower their standards, 40, 139
  for publishers to make their work OA, 121–122, 145, 159
  for search engines to index OA repositories, 57
Indian Institute of Science, 30
Information overload, 120–121, 205nn23–24
Ingelfinger rule, 173
Ingenta, 147
Inger, Simon, 157, 216n8
Institute of Physics (IOP), 151, 215n2
International Association of Scientific, Technical and Medical Publishers (STM), 184n12, 207–208n2
International Center for Tropical Agriculture, 195–196n12
International Communication Association, 191n20
International Conference on Electronic Theses and Dissertations, 199n4
Internet, 1, 7, 9, 109
  access to, 7, 25, 48, 116 (*see also* Digital divide)
  Budapest Open Access Initiative and, 19
  generational change and, 164–165
  makes OA possible, 1, 9, 19–20
  peer review and, 165–166
  widens distribution and reduces costs, 44
ISI Citation Database, 187n2

Markets, 10, 12, 13, 38–39, 41, 44,
130, 184n14. *See also* Mo-
nopolies and anti-competitive
practices
Massachusetts Institute of Technol-
ogy (MIT), 82, 181n2, 194n7
McAfee, Preston, 183n9, 184n15
McMillan, Gail, 199n4
McPherson, Isaac, 46
McPherson, James, 33, 138n10
McVeigh, Marie E., 187n2
Medknow, 159, 212n14, 216n10
Mendeley, 173, 218n7
Merck Company Foundation,
197–198n20
Metadata, 81–82, 110
Milloy, Caren, 200–201n8
Minho University, 194n8
Misunderstandings, x, 52, 54, 55,
56, 58, 71, 72, 88, 89, 99–100,
103, 111, 137–140, 163–168,
189n9, 192–193n4, 217n3
Mitchell, Anne, 208n4
Molecular Biology of the Cell (journal),
159
Monographs. *See* Books
Monopolies and anti-competitive
practices, 32, 33, 38, 39–40, 130
(*see also* Markets)
Moral hazard, 41, 185n18
Morris, Chris, 208n4
Morris, Sally, 184n15
Morrison, Heather, 213n18
Morrison, James, 205n22
Movies and moviemakers, 8, 9,
12–13, 20
Music and musicians, 8, 9, 12–13, 20

Napier University, 195–196n12

National Academies Press, 109–110,
201n9
National Institutes of Health (NIH).
See also Funding; Funding agencies; Mandates
copyright and, 126, 128
green OA and, 150, 152, 155, 157
OA (or "public access") policy, 72,
80, 83–88, 126, 128, 150, 180n1,
188n4, 191n19, 195nn9–10,
197n19, 206n1, 206n3, 214n1,
215nn3–4, 216n7
National Library of Medicine, 117,
204n17
National Science Laboratory, China,
195–196n12
National University of Ireland,
208–209n4
Nature Publishing Group (NPG),
154–155, 216n6
Neston, Shannon, 194n7
Newspapers, 98. *See also* Journalism
and journalists
Next Generation Learning Challenges, 197–198n20
Nonrivalrous property, 45–48
Novels and novelists, 9, 12–13, 17,
98, 130–131

Oberlin College, 194n7
Office of System wide Library Plan-
ning, 181n2
O'Leary, Brian, 200–201n8
Onsrud, Harlan, xii
Open access. *See also* Access; Gold
OA (through journals); Gratis
OA; Green OA (through reposi-
tories); Impact; Libre OA; Open-
access journals and publishers

gold OA and, 77–79, 83–84, 91–93, 134, 192–193n4

gratis OA and, 71–72

green OA and, 59, 77–79, 83–84, 93, 149, 161

historical timing and, 71–73, 90–95

libre OA and, 72, 90–91, 93

mandates and, 54, 58–59, 63, 78–95, 149–157, 174, 192n2, 192–193n4

permission and, 79–83, 84, 90, 93

repositories and, 77, 79–83, 86–87, 174

SHERPA and, 171

universities and, 4, 23, 59, 71–72, 77–87, 90, 128, 149–150, 172–173, 192n2

waivers and, 80–84, 87–94, 155

Postprints. *See also* Peer review; Preprints; Versions

gold OA and, 60, 100

green OA and, 60, 100, 173, 199n2

peer review and, 99–104, 173

Poynder, Richard, 178n3, 186n20, 189n10, 189–190n12, 200n5, 202–203n14

Preprints, 114. *See also* Ingelfinger rule; Peer review; Postprints; Versions

green OA and, 60, 63, 100, 173

peer review and, 20–21, 52, 98–104

Preservation, 6, 34, 52, 62, 63, 74, 102, 136, 167

Prestige, 16, 40, 50, 54–55, 60–61, 84, 167, 169–170, 171. *See also* Authors; Career-building for faculty; Impact; Journals (in

general); Open-access journals and publishers; Toll-access (or conventional) journals and publishers

Prices. *See* Access; Toll-access (or conventional) journals and publishers

Print, 1, 18, 34, 35, 47, 108–111, 137, 144, 166, 167. *See also* Books; Digitization

print-era models, 18, 111, 144

print-on-demand (POD), 108

rivalrous, 47–48

Processing, 5–6, 44, 120–123. *See also* Machines; Search and search engines; Text mining

Promotion and tenure, 13, 60, 86, 130, 195–196n12. *See also* Career-building for faculty; Prestige; Universities

Public domain, 21, 69, 99, 111, 125, 190n17. *See also* Copyright; Libre OA

Public Knowledge, xi

Public Knowledge Project, 143

Public Library of Science, 142, 212n14

Publishers. *See* Open-access journals and publishers; Societies, scholarly; Toll-access (or conventional) journals and publishers

Publishers Association (PA), 207–208n2

Publishing (in general). *See also* Open-access journals and publishers; Toll-access (or conventional) journals and publishers

added value, 35, 142–143, 145

costs, 21–22, 119, 142–144

Publishing and the Ecology of European Research (PEER), 189n9, 215n4

Publishing Research Consortium (PRC), 134, 157–158

PubMed Central, 57, 188n7. *See also* Repositories

Queensland University of Technology, 193n6

Queen's University, 192n3

Rausing, Lisbet, xii

Readers. *See* Lay readers; Researchers

Referees. *See also* Peer review
  fee waivers and, 139, 170
  generally not paid by journals, 17–18, 19, 20, 25, 37, 44, 142, 184n13
  incentives for, 19
  networks to find, 103
  preprints and, 21, 98
  standards and, 104
  value adders, 37

Registry of Open Access Repositories (ROAR), 188n6, 192n2, 218n6, 219

Registry of Open Access Repository Material Archiving Policies (ROARMAP), 192n2, 193n4, 219

Repositories, 49, 52, 67, 111. *See also* ArXiv; Dark deposits; Green OA (OA through repositories); Open Archives Initiative (OAI); PubMed Central; Self-archiving
  contents, variety of, 52, 134–136, 173–174

costs, 51, 53, 59, 62, 134, 136, 208–209n4

dark deposits and, 52, 81–82

disciplinary, 57, 173 (*see also* ArXiv; PubMed Central)

institutional, 57, 80, 86, 134–136, 173

interoperable, 56–57

peer review and, 51–53, 64, 171

policies and, 77, 79–83, 86–87, 174

purposes of, 134–135

unfamiliarity with, 52, 55, 58

universal repositories, 173

Research. *See also* Harm to research or researchers; Knowledge; Mandates; Policies; Processing; Researchers
  grants and, 13–14, 23, 80–84, 88, 129, 150, 170
  growth of published research, 41–43, 64
  inquiry and truth-seeking, 10–12, 13, 14, 112–115, 120–121
  libraries and, 30–32, 35, 40–41, 141, 146, 156–157, 160
  policies and, 78–89, 93–95
  public interests served by, ix, 14
  as wider category than knowledge, 112–115

Research Councils UK, 155

Researchers. *See also* Authors; Harm to research or researchers; Lay readers
  as authors, 2–4, 9–12, 15–17, 25, 77, 102
  as readers, 15, 25, 40–41, 102, 119
  unfamiliarity with OA, x, 40–41, 55, 58, 77

197n17, 217n3. *See also* Mandates; Policies; Universities

Universal access, 26–27

Universities. *See also* Libraries; Mandates; Policies; Promotion and tenure; Repositories; Theses and dissertations; Unanimous faculty votes

libraries and, 32, 42, 111, 147, 174

mandates, 79–90, 96, 149 (*see also* Mandates)

paying publication fees, 136, 139, 145, 147, 170, 210–211n11, 214n19

policies, 4, 23, 59, 71–72, 77–87, 90, 94, 128, 129, 149–150, 172–173 (*see also* Policies)

public funding for public purpose of, 14, 38–39

salaries and, 12, 14, 17

as stakeholders in OA, x, 77–78

upstream from publishers, 129

usefulness or utility of research, ix, 5, 6, 40, 75, 102, 115, 121–123

University College London, 193n5

University of Athabasca, 192n3

University of Bielefeld, 192n3

University of Calgary, 210n11

University of California, 181n2, 186n22

University of Chicago, 200–201n8

University of Ghent, 193n5

University of Hawaii-Manoa, 194n7

University of Hong Kong, 194n6

University of Kansas, 194n7

University of Liège, 194n6, 195–196n12

University of Maine, xi

University of Memphis, 202n13

University of Minho, 193n6

University of Northern Colorado Libraries, 194n6

University of Oregon, 192n3, 194n7

University of Oregon Department of Romance Languages, 194n7, 195–196n12

University of Oregon Library Faculty, 194n7

University of Pretoria, 194n6

University of Puerto Rico Law School, 194n7

University of Salford, 194n6

University of Sassari, 192n3, 197–198n20

University of Strathclyde, 193n5

University of Tampere, 192n3

University of Utrecht, 192n3

University of Virginia, 192n3

University of Washington, 192n3

University of Westminster, 193n5

University of Zurich, 193n5

U.S. Congress, 72, 152, 187n24

U.S. Department of Education, 197–198n20

U.S. Department of Health and Human Services, 197–198n20

U.S. Department of Homeland Security, 197–198n20

U.S. Department of Labor, 197–198n20

U.S. Department of State, 197–198n20

U.S. Institute of Medicine, 197–198n20

Varmus, Harold, 187n24

Velterop, Jan, 41, 145, 185n18, 196n13, 213n17